The Secret Beliefs of The Illuminati: The Complete Truth About Manifesting Money Using The Law of Attraction That is Being Hidden From You

Dan Desmarques

Published by 22 Lions Publishing, 2020.

Table of Contents

Copyright Page..1

Book Reviews...3

Introduction...5

Chapter 1: The Transference...7

Chapter 2: The Dual Perspective...11

Chapter 3: The 11 Levels of Awakening...13

Chapter 4: The 6 Layers of Hidden Knowledge....................................15

Chapter 5: Zen...19

Chapter 6: Influence..21

Chapter 7: The Alchemic Cycles...25

Chapter 8: Resilience...27

Chapter 9: The Transition From Knowledge to Awareness................31

Chapter 10: The Self-Deception...35

Chapter 11: The Transition From Awareness to Power......................37

Chapter 12: Truthfulness and Power...41

Chapter 13: The Bridge Between Heart and Mind..............................45

Chapter 14: How Passion Attracts Love..47

Chapter 15: The Fluidity of Thought...51

Chapter 16: The Relationship Between Moral and Money.................55

Chapter 17: The Relationship Between Moral and Success................59

Chapter 18: The Relationship Between Money and Love...................63

Chapter 19: Why You Shouldn't Hate The Truth. 65

Chapter 20: God and Courage. 67

Chapter 21: We Are One. 69

Chapter 22: Positive Thinking. 71

Chapter 23: Immortality. 73

Chapter 24: The Development of Superhuman Abilities. 75

Chapter 25: The Purpose of The Law of Attraction. 79

Chapter 26: Things They Don't Want You to Know. 83

Chapter 27: How People Suppress Their Potential. 87

Chapter 28: How Powerful Can a Human Be? 91

Chapter 29: How Fast Can You Change? 95

Chapter 30: The Relationship Between Action and Consciousness. 97

Chapter 31: The Perception of Failure. 101

Chapter 32: Faith. 103

Chapter 33: The Predisposition For Failure. 105

Chapter 34: Why People Don't Change? 109

Chapter 35: How to Escape Your Illusions. 113

Chapter 36: The Path of Purification. 117

Chapter 37: How The Truth Was Hidden. 121

Chapter 38: The Path of The Heart. 123

Chapter 39: How to Move Between Parallel Realities. 127

Chapter 40: The Challenges of Transfiguration. 129

Chapter 41: The Miracles of Life.. 131

Chapter 42: Cosmic Consciousness.. 135

Chapter 43: How to Perceive The Physical World...................................... 139

Chapter 44: The Sexual Energy... 143

Chapter 45: Why The Truth Remains Hidden.. 147

Chapter 46: How to Know Yourself.. 151

Chapter 47: What is Fear?... 155

Chapter 48: The Fundamental Difference in Humans............................... 159

Chapter 49: Your Spiritual DNA... 163

Chapter 50: The Source.. 167

Chapter 51: Spiritual Frequencies... 171

Chapter 52: How to Maintain a Higher Frequency?.................................. 175

Chapter 53: Truth Has Its Own Frequency... 179

Chapter 54: The Real Spiritual Battle... 183

Chapter 55: The Energy of Nature.. 185

Chapter 56: How a Spiritual Life Makes You Rich..................................... 187

Chapter 57: Human Development and Spirituality................................... 189

Chapter 58: The Frequency of a Culture.. 193

Chapter 59: Recognizing Danger and Love... 197

Chapter 60: How the Subconscious Determines Your Fate....................... 201

Chapter 61: How to Assimilate Your Emotions.. 205

Chapter 62: Earthing Therapy... 209

Chapter 63: Why We Are What We Eat. 213

Chapter 64: How Frequencies Heal The Body. 217

Chapter 65: The Plan to Enslave of Humankind. 221

Chapter 66: What Future Can We Expect? 223

Chapter 67: TransHumanism. 225

Chapter 68: The World We Could Have. 229

Chapter 69: How to Develop Self-Control. 231

Chapter 70: Should You Be Superstitious? 233

Chapter 71: Can Your Friends Determine Your Future? 235

Chapter 72: Success is a Lonely Road. 237

Chapter 73: How to Become a Magnet to Success. 241

Chapter 74: Emotions and Money. 245

Chapter 75: The Potential to Become Wealthy. 249

Chapter 76: The Social Implications of TransHumanism. 253

Chapter 77: Why Thoughts Differentiate Potential. 257

Chapter 78: The Willingness to Learn. 261

Chapter 79: What Economy Teaches About Society. 263

Chapter 80: The Impact of Our Social Paradigms. 267

Chapter 81: Perspective and Relativity. 271

Chapter 82: Most People Will Die With Their Dreams. 275

Chapter 83: Wealth is Always Relative to Location. 277

Chapter 84: Love or Money? 279

Chapter 85: Absurd Facts About Money. 281

Chapter 86: The Alchemical Transmutation. 285

Chapter 87: What Happens When You Surrender to God? 287

Chapter 88: Haters Will Hate! 289

Chapter 89: God is Your Best Companion. 291

Chapter 90: The Path of Self-Destruction. 293

Chapter 91: Time and Transmutation. 295

Chapter 92: Why You Must Serve God. 297

Chapter 93: God Helps Those Who Help Themselves. 299

Chapter 94: The Path of Darkness. 301

Chapter 95: How to Deprogram Yourself. 305

Chapter 96: Delusional and Realistic Dreams. 309

Chapter 97: How Your Attitude Can Make You Wealthy. 311

Chapter 98: Help Creates Bridges Towards Your Dreams. 313

Chapter 99: How to Reprogram Emotional Responses. 317

Chapter 100: The Process of Becoming Self-Aware. 321

Chapter 101: Exercises of Mind-Control. 325

Chapter 102: How to Control Your Thoughts. 329

Chapter 103: How to Overcome Your Painful Memories. 331

Chapter 104: The Illusion of a Timeline. 335

Chapter 105: Why Some People Reject Help? 337

Chapter 106: Those Who Choose to Live in Bubbles of Illusion. 341

Chapter 107: Where Are Our Prophets? 343

Chapter 108: The Challenges of Faith. 345

Chapter 109: The Truth Will Set You Free. 347

Chapter 110: The True Cause of Death. 349

Chapter 111: Important Quotes to Remember. 351

Chapter 112: Bibliography. 367

Chapter 113: Additional Resources... 373

Book Review Request 375

Other Books Written By The Author... 377

Copyright Page

The Secret Beliefs of The Illuminati: The Complete Truth About Manifesting Money Using The Law of Attraction That Is Being Hidden From You

By Dan Desmarques

Copyright © Dan Desmarques, 2012 (1st Ed.) All Rights Reserved.

Copyright © Dan Desmarques, 2014 (2nd Ed.) All Rights Reserved.

Copyright © Dan Desmarques, 2014 (3rd Ed.) All Rights Reserved.

Copyright © Dan Desmarques, 2015 (4th Ed.) All Rights Reserved.

Copyright © Dan Desmarques, 2020 (5th Ed.) All Rights Reserved.

Book Reviews.

"Awesome book! Not what you might expect. If you get your spirituality correct, your physical needs will be provided by the unseen power of the universe." —Tom Caldwell

"Expands your mind to all possibilities and to discover the truths of how we function in this world, and how you can control your mind and guide it to the right places you desire." —Alejandro Meza

"I lost my way after my niece died two years ago and now I'm encouraged to see the world in a different light." —Jaci Oj

"This book really opened my eyes. I learned to be more spiritual and to be more patient with the world." —Martha Pelletier

"This book is truly a great read! I'm glad I purchased it, for it contains great knowledge and wisdom. I highly recommend! It will make you view life differently and help in bringing awareness to your own personal spiritual journey." —Dimitri Stupak

"This book will surely open your mind to greater possibilities for your spirit, body and mind." —Tiffany Top

"Truly opened my eyes! These steps are really enlightening!" —Sevor Klu

"This book will change you positively. It helped me at many levels." —Jeff Ureta

"Brilliant! Truly enlightening! Love it!" —Juan José de Díos Zapata

"Great Read! This book changed my life." —Terez Flanagan

"It gets you to read it again and again." —Kazama Muramasa

Introduction.

The world keeps changing extremely fast, but in times of abundance and scarcity, under revolutions or wars, many have prospered. And they did so by looking at the patterns of reality. They understood these Divine Patterns and used them to achieve their personal goals.

The patterns have been kept secret for thousands of years in religious books, manuscripts and even fairytales, under allegories and metaphors meant to hide them in plain sight.

The enlightened ones — those who can see, called that Sacred Geometry, in a direct reference to the Creator. They then studied the nature of life through the art of the Almighty God, the Master Architect of the Universe. For "The secret of the occult sciences is that of nature itself" (Albert Pike, Freemason).

They discovered that there is only one Truth, one God and one religion, despite the many branches characterizing the impulses of the masses.

They also saw that this Truth is manifested by the highest moral state, from which the highest wisdom is received. That is when "the half-told story comes to be finished" (Arthur Conan Doyle, Freemason).

The one who completes these studies becomes a master of the craft, for he possesses the capacity to alter reality with his mind, and create new worlds like a mason or builder. He becomes both aware and responsible of what he experiences, as much as he is made able to transition to new momentums and alter the future. For "When the Mason learns that the key is a proper application of the dynamo of living power, he has learned the mystery of the craft" (Manly P. Hall, Freemason).

This great secret was reorganized here to show you exactly how to experience it, and despite the many attempts of others to remove this knowledge from the public eye.

This information comes now as a great opportunity for you to transcend into a new perspective on the attraction of wealth.

Chapter 1: The Transference.

The law of attraction is just the tip of the iceberg on the amount of power that everyone possesses within themselves to change anything.

It all starts with our perspective of the world. In truth, the law of attraction cannot be fully understood without an acknowledgement of the social programming and how the power elite became so powerful, or how they keep such power.

There has been a transference of power and symbols from culture to culture, while the masses were kept in the dark, indoctrinated into falsehood and manipulated through religion. "It's called transference. It's very common in symbology. The Nazis took the swastika from the Hindus, the Christians adopted the cruciform from the Egyptians" (Dan Brown, In Angels & Demons).

The light got clearer and the darkness got darker, and two groups in our world expanded in either enlightenment or ignorance.

Today we can go much deeper than our symbols, when we begin analyzing our ideas about money and wealth, or our values and needs, as well as our priorities and dreams.

The gap is so wide, that one feels like his personality is being thorn apart when uncovering the truth. But "Nothing exists except through human consciousness" (George Orwell, Freemason).

You can't really make significant changes in your physical existence if they're incompatible with your belief system. Your beliefs shape the patterns of energy in which you live, and keep you there permanently, unless you transform.

Any ritual that intends to guide you out of this prison, has to create a rupture within you, between your emotions, thoughts, beliefs and attachments. Because you can only attract new and more effective ideas when they don't match your preexistent mental patterns.

Here we have the meaning of resurrection, not as a mystical or religious restart but rather a reformation of the personality, and more precisely, your heart and outward conduct.

The expansion on the amount of opportunities for change and reformation is proportional to the rightful knowledge acquired.

One must know before he can be. But because the universal is made with dualities, he must decide what he wants to be, before he can know what he must know. If you do not know what you must know, your life is guided by default patterns.

As the poor do not know what they must know, and allow themselves to absorb what the rich want them to know, both their entertainment and salary are provided by the rich, and end up complementing one another in a form of mental enslavement.

The one who does not know is always slave to that which is known. Reason why "poor people have a big TV and rich people have a big library" (Jim Rohn, Freemason).

If one then awakens to the possibility of acquiring something greater to himself, he must necessarily revolt against the system and his conditions. That has the name of self-education.

A governmental education can't provide the means to escape the same system that it promotes. That would be a conflict of its own interests. Reason why teachers and professors who get confused about their role, and promote this rebellion through the proper exercise of thought, are removed from their position.

Many times, this occurs through the most indoctrinated among their students, that despite not yet having graduated, are already brainwashed enough to protect their own prison of thought.

As thought is always a product of socialization, a self-education cannot, as well, be driven by what is popular or recommended. For that is a preselection made from the masses who are asleep.

Your decisions must become independent and driven by your higher self, in order for you to become a mason of your own life.

Chapter 2: The Dual Perspective.

We always behave according to what we believe. Therefore, we can't see that which is found outside our spectrum of possibilities. We can only see what we think we are seeing. And we form our patterns of reason accordingly.

The outside world then reflects the inner world, both in a mentally ill person and in the one who is sane.

However, it is the sane one who can look at himself from the perspective of reality where he finds himself.

He then understands the elements that are found in both worlds, such as the concept of value. For "You don't get paid for the hour but for the value you bring to the hour" (Jim Rohn, Freemason).

The same mental exercise allows seeing that you never attract money but lessons to understand it instead, through hard work and experiences of a new nature — the intermediate process to change your thoughts about money, and before changing the reality of scarcity.

The same principle is seen when you want to attract love, cars, vacations and job opportunities:

- Without self-love, you'll attract someone that invalidates you;

- Without a purpose for the car, you may soon crash it in an accident;

- Job opportunities will teach you about the importance of self-respect and life goals;

- Vacations will teach you the importance of perspective, between the state of work and leisure.

Ideally, you want to be part of a reality where the contrast of perspectives, or gap between energies, is nullified, because then you can channel your energy fully to the attraction of wealth.

You do this by shifting your thoughts on what I just mentioned:

- You find a spouse who admires you and respects your goals in life;

- You buy a car that is useful for you, even if for your self-esteem only;

- You choose a career in which you have pleasure in your work;

- You choose to live in the same location where you would go on vacations.

We are always attracting our future but by default and with irresponsibility.

In this process, we normally attract problems to learn more about ourselves. But we avoid the confrontation, refuse the responsibility and point fingers at others.

In doing so, we keep repeating the same cycles until the lessons are learned.

If we do not learn from our experiences, we may succumb to fear, depression and an overall downgrade of our motivation. We then stop dreaming and become apathetic.

With such state of mind, we will tend to assimilate the values that keep us there, such as the widespread beliefs of the masses.

The opposite comes from an acceptance of the challenges which are necessary to change our condition. "Happiness can exist only in acceptance" (George Orwell, Freemason).

Chapter 3: The 11 Levels of Awakening.

Our life is predictable because we only wish that which we are supposed to wish, as we can't wish that which we can't see.

As people typically feel safe within patterns of predictability, to be unpredictable is then to be found crazy by those who are predictable.

It is also to step out of the cycle in which they plant their own truths.

This new state of mind, requires a direction and an energy of its own, which comes from the process itself.

The key to such change is then in the decision made when combined with the direction, more than it is in the information.

The information will be attracted by the intended focus, resulting from the decision making when merging with the new direction — key and lock.

The levels experienced afterwards, result from the natural process of awakening:

- Knowledge: Insights and perceptions leading to awareness;

- Awareness: A light of consciousness showing us a potential force;

- Potential: The channeled energies that indicate doors of opportunity;

- Opportunity: An intersection of the physical and non-physical universes that aligns with creativity;

- Creativity: The art of changing reality with our thoughts that leads to inspiration;

- Inspiration: A channeling from the realm of ideas that reveals the tools we need;

- Ideas: Inspired communication received from the Divine Realm of Truth;

- Truthfulness: A neutral, non-judgmental, way of seeing that leads us to power;

- Power: The capacity to achieve and transform;

- Transformation: The alchemical process that leads us to spiritual wisdom;

- Wisdom: A state of understanding by seeing and channeling through Divine Consciousness.

When trying to apply the law of attraction, many people are stopped before the first step — the insights. And that is why they fail in getting to their results, even when reading abundantly and accumulating a vast amount of knowledge.

This occurs because they perceive reality from a single perspective — the "me", or ego.

In order for one to acquire awareness through knowledge, one must perceive knowledge beyond himself. After that, layers of subtle information are revealed, all of which describe different states of awareness.

The greater your awareness, the more able you are to unveil the many layers present in a book or even a conversation.

Chapter 4: The 6 Layers of Hidden Knowledge.

There are 6 layers for the hidden knowledge in all of creation, and they can be seen when we form a line of communication with the object of our observation.

If the object of observation is a book...

- **The First Layer** are the words, which can only be understood if you already have a meaning for them. That meaning comes first from the use of the word in your life, then the use of this word in the life of others, and finally the extension of the word in terms of emotional meanings for the author;

- **The Second Layer** are the patterns, which reveal structures of thought processes. These structures will merge with your own, to then allow forming a relationship with the author. If you can develop empathy for the author, you will be able to know his mind;

- **The Third Layer** comes as an empathic relationship with the universe of the author, which allows seeing the world as he sees it, and not only as he describes it. Through this exercise, you will be able to develop what is called a "non-judgmental judgement". For you will see in the author things that he may not even see in himself or his life — his own spiritual experience or path;

- **The Fourth Layer** is the spiritual experience of merging your mind with that of the author himself. You will not lose your identity but rather expand your divine state of being, by being able to feel what someone, that may not even be alive anymore, feels;

- **The Fifth Layer** is the awareness itself, a state of blissfulness, in which you lose the sense of time, space or spiritual differentiation. You and the author become one and the same. You can see that he is not you, and yet you can see life as if living through his body.

- **The Sixth Layer** is the maintenance of the state of blissfulness, or in other words, the state of being without being, knowing without knowing and acting without acting. It is a state that Zen Buddhists have described abundantly, but is often misunderstood in the western world as some form of passive living. The zen state or sixth layer, is not about being passive or absent from life, but rather becoming life itself with full awareness, and in a state of permanent consciousness.

You will know your self and your state, when you are able to apply what I have just described — and that you can practice with the act of reading consciously — when with others. Because, there are two types of living as there are two types of reading:

- **Those who read with their mind remain blind** — They see only words and can merely debate interpretations. The Truth is veiled before their eyes;

- **The ones who can read with their heart** — These are loved by God because they practice the true religion. This true religion is cosmic consciousness, a method of awakening through empathy, rejection of dogma and the embracing of a higher perception in relation to possibilities.

We instinctively know the importance of this cosmic consciousness but can rarely see it, unless we are confronted with the other — that what is and is not at the same time.

This condition is present in our reality as it is present in the state of being of others. We may call it good and bad, or one opinion versus another opinion, one perspective opposing another perspective, but is just consciousness trying to reveal itself within us.

If we wish to adopt this type of consciousness in our daily interactions, we necessarily need to understand zen, but it is just the first stage.

Chapter 5: Zen.

Eventually, we will have to learn to act without acting, defend without attacking, and win without the need to win.

This application has been widely applied by masters of the Japanese martial arts but can be used in a debate, as much as it can be used for combat.

- **Acting without acting**, is to reposition your body or argument in such a way that your opponent is not prepared to defend himself and is forced to react by not reacting;

- **Defending without defending**, is to control the mind of your opponent in such a way that he is demotivated, and it can be done through intimidation as much as it can be done with a smile;

- **Winning without the need to win**, comes only when you either master the art of combat, and can neutralize your opponent without the need to prove something, or take his life, or when your consciousness of reality is such, that you can defeat any argument without the need to be right about what you say. The use of scientific facts and historical examples is a common way of doing this. For you are not projecting your ego into your argument when applying this principle.

Ideally, one should come to such a state of awareness in which,...

- **Acting without acting**, means to be where the reality surrounding you uplifts you, rather than opposes you. A religion, a family, a club or society, and even a business partnership have this purpose;

- **Defending without defending**, means to reposition yourself in space and reorganize your life in such a way, that your past becomes merely a memory. This typically occurs when you make your culture and experiences obsolete, by moving to a new location. Even a walk in the park can help you distance yourself from the things that trouble your mind, and help you relax;

- **Winning without winning**, becomes the joy of competing, overcoming challenges, and seeking problems, simply because you are in love with your life and everyone that surrounds you. This is made possible for the one who has found pleasure in work, pleasure in learning from different viewpoints, and pleasure in the act of creating and achieving goals.

If you can develop yourself in such a way, that what I just described becomes natural to you, you will not suffer from depression, loneliness or even the fear of what others think and dead itself.

Taking into consideration that over 90% of the mental illnesses, and even physical illnesses, are psychosomatic, it is easy to come to the conclusion that this knowledge will improve your overall well-being.

As a spiritual creature, your health depends on the acknowledgment of your spiritual needs, and not only physical.

You need love, happiness and security, as much as you need food, exercise and water.

Chapter 6: Influence.

The spiritual levels of awakening that one experiences, will then reorganize the way of living. And ideally, we should be able to apply the same principles in our daily interactions with others.

- **Knowledge:** When you understand the person in front of you, through communication;

- **Awareness:** The communication with another leads you to see the potential for a friendship or not. And, you can actually measure this by how another interacts with you, namely, by the amount of similar goals, similar viewpoints, and the affinity created or how another person feels about you;

- **Potential:** Our interactions open new doors, namely, when you find something pleasant and new about another person, that can be interesting for you to learn or experience;

- **Opportunity:** Here, the intersection of the physical and non-physical, that aligns with creativity, is found in the things that the other shows you and you did not know or considered to exist. It can even be a new friendship or a romance, as when one friend of the same gender as us, takes us to a party, where we meet another friend of the same gender, that then invites us to meet him and his wife, and his wife happens to have a single friend, that meets with her that same day and falls in love with us. It can also occur through us seeking for a hairdresser, and eventually finding one that develops a relationship with us. Or even as business opportunities, that come years later, through the students that a teacher was working with, and that never forgot how much he did for them;

- **Creativity:** The art of changing reality with our thoughts comes precisely from the interaction with new realities emerging from new opportunities;

- **Inspiration:** We become more inspired whenever we act according to what God gives us. This means respecting the person offering us a job opportunity that we wanted for a long time, appreciating the love of someone we were trying to find for many years, and putting the efforts to comprehend someone who wants to develop a business idea with us, or help us develop our own;

- **Ideas:** An inspired communication becomes an honest communication, when you are appreciative of your interactions. The words flow through you without a need for analysis or even thinking. It becomes a spontaneous conversation, flowing between your connectedness with the spiritual world and the physical world, in which what you say isn't as important as what you feel that you must or must not say;

- **Truthfulness:** It is an art in the act of having a conversation with a neutral, and non-judgmental, way of seeing the other person, and that leads us to power — influence;

- **Power:** The capacity to achieve agreements, and transform the views of another person through a positive approach to life — it is to uplift another;

- **Transformation:** The alchemical process of exchanging emotions with another person and uplift him or her, eventually leading us to more wisdom, about us, the other and life itself;

- **Wisdom:** A state of understanding by seeing and channeling through Divine Consciousness, while interacting with the people that are within our spectrum of reality.

As you develop these qualities and skills, you will turn into a better version of yourself, and a more pleasant human being as well. Others will want to be around you, they will invite you to spend time with them, they will take you to meet their own friends, and in time, you will be loved by many that will want to talk to you, help you and uplift your existence.

When this happens, the law of attraction is under the control of your vibration, your own consciousness, and basically, you.

This you, is the one who has decided everything already, and is now attracting the same future that he has envisioned in the past.

You will then see the poles and levels closing the gap between themselves, and merging with one another, to lead you to what I explained as being a neutral way of living, or zen, in which you act without acting.

Chapter 7: The Alchemic Cycles.

The three upper levels of consciousness — power, transformation and wisdom —will become one with the three lower levels — knowledge, awareness and potential.

In other words, you become powerful as an influencer, you transform others with your divine presence, you are wise in your words and actions, and as a result, you are offered knowledge, a higher awareness of the many opportunities that seem to appear out of nowhere, and potential to acquire more.

In return, the knowledge, awareness and potential of the ones you interact with, will influence you, transform you and make you wiser.

In the middle — the balance of the opposing forces — that can actually be seen as gradients, you find inspiration: You will know, not based on what you think, but what is fact through what works for you, what makes you succeed beyond your capacity to be able to explain such success.

Many seek for shortcuts to what I have just describe, by joining specific secret societies, but the ignorance of what I described blinds them. For God does not allow for enlightenment to the ones who are not prepared to receive it and even violate His Laws.

Many are unable to perceive with the heart that which they see with their mind. Because God has made them blind.

As a result, these seekers of truth now have to humble themselves and merge with the bottom layer to find their path again.

This is how God has hidden the truth — He revealed it to the authors, the virtuous who are leaders of new religions of their own, and the communities that have separated themselves from the whole of the social system to form their own ideology and live by their own values.

As the top of the pyramid became corrupted, the truth was moved to the bottom, so that the cycle of transformation, from the upper layer to the bottom layer and vice-versa, may occur.

This is the reason why alchemy can only occur through cycles of spiritual rebellion, transformation and a rupture with the past, eventually leading to its renovation.

We necessarily need to destroy the old religions to form new ones, which, by revealing the truths of the old, and segregating themselves from their lies, emerge as new opportunities for those who want to understand God.

Surely, not all religions are aligned with what I just said. But if they are, they will not proclaim to be unique, but rather a branch of the one Truth in the Tree of Knowledge.

No religion is supreme to the Truth or a reflection of such Truth, but rather a reflection of the need for unity and development.

Chapter 8: Resilience.

A large amount of people that try to follow the spiritual laws, either when described by religion or independent authors, fail and then quit.

In every situation I encountered, I have found that this happens because they lack knowledge on the intermediary steps, I.e., they don't know how to transform themselves between one stage of spiritual development and the next.

As they are completely immersed within their mind, controlled by their ego, can only understand in a direct correlation with their needs. If such needs are not satisfied, they become blind to the rest of the information.

It is a very infantile way of looking at reality. It means that such individuals think like little children, and cannot perceive reality as adults.

As such, they don't really understand what to be a mature adult means. They lack the skills to act in a social manner, because they cannot not act like a toddler.

A child wants things out of need, but does not acquire the perception of the need of others, not until he is 4 or 5 years old. Until then, he does not possess social cognition.

The same occurs with those who want to be rich or famous, but can't understand that, in order to be rich, one must produce something of value to others, and to be famous, they must acquire a level of competence in personality, attributes or skills, that is admired by many.

Object permanence, or the understanding that objects continue to exist, even when they cannot be seen, is another topic that has been researched abundantly, and again, shows us the mental development of an individual.

A Swiss psychologist named Piaget, concluded that it is only around 12 months that a child is able to retrieve an object that was hidden from sight. Before that, a baby makes no attempt to retrieve it.

Interestingly, we see the same pattern in adults, for after being demoralized, lose interest in pursuing what they want, in this case, an object which is the goal of their desire.

As we compare these experiments with adult behavior, we see that it is possible to bring anyone to an infantile state through the demoralization process, e.g., giving and taking something away from the individual.

The one who succeeds has to then, and necessarily, fight against a stream of occurrences, merging culture, social habits, education, and trends.

Only then can he become resilient enough to achieve his goals, through the process of attempt and failure.

The capacity to overcome failure is then a predisposition developed through resilience, that can only be obtained when we develop a determined mind.

Everything that an entrepreneur faces — abandonment, ridicule, rejection, failure, disappointment, and betrayal, are part of this stream of energy that I am showing here.

When his goals are aligned with the stream, the energy necessary to overcome the resistance of this flow, is necessarily much higher.

For example:

- He meets a woman who is obsessed with social validation and falls in love with her;

- He is struggling to be accepted by his family and they don't understand what he does;

- He wants to maintain a healthy social life but the habits of his friends conflict with his own goals.

It is said that leaders and successful entrepreneurs are very lonely people, and as I have seen, this is true, but not by their own choice.

Entrepreneurs enjoy debating ideas, meeting new people and learning new things. But they are aware of this stream of emotional pressure coming from others, and usually, can only relax around those who are appreciative or have a similar way of thinking.

If we wish to diminish the force of this stream coming form the outside world, we need to focus on the stream of energy coming from within, and that means developing our determinism through an emotional force that comes from love.

- Love for life;
- Love for what we do;
- Love for who we are;
- Love for what our goals mean to us;
- Love for the process of transformation.

This love for the alchemical transmutation, is what the gnostic teachings, and in particular, the Nag Hammadi Library, and the teachings of Jesus in particular, show us.

Chapter 9: The Transition From Knowledge to Awareness.

When people acquire knowledge and can't understand its application, they will fail to gain awareness.

Such is the case of what happens in the various Educational Institutions, and in particular, Universities.

College students are taught to repeat processes, and quite often, they don't even understand how such processes were invented, or what makes them useful.

They are exposed to an abundance of information that must be replicated but can't really be debated.

It is not the job of the student to question the validity of the information received.

As such, many of them never acquire a proper awareness of the mechanics in their thought process, and which emerge from this brainwashing, this assimilation of patterns without a comprehension.

They become educated morons — able to think thoughts that are not their own.

The educational system has succeeded, throughout the entire world, in creating a whole lineage of students that...

- Can't think, when they think they are thinking;

- Can't argue, when they think they are arguing;

- Can't introspect their own behavior, while believing to be introspecting their behavior;

- Can't analyze data, when assuming they are analyzing data;

- Can't empathize with those who are not similar to them in some way, or cooperate with them, but compete.

As such, they become immersed in a trance, and don't seem to understand why they will never get what they want from life by looking at the outside rather than the inside — their own unnatural state of awareness.

- They want money but don't understand anything about money;

- They want success but disregard the importance of values leading to admiration;

- They want to be popular but only because they crave egotistic attention.

Since the end of the 80s and beginning of the 90s, the ones in power, that, in many cases, care about nobody but themselves, have found ways to implement communist ideals in the masses, by studying their weaknesses and psychological tendencies, by looking into their behavior patterns and taking advantage of their fears and needs. And so, we have now before us, a whole world full of infantile idiots, who are absolutely convinced that their ideals are truly uplifting and worthwhile.

They cannot understand anything beyond their version of reality. They even see as a personal attack any attempt at correcting them.

They are useless, except as a tool of the system that has made them.

They will fight for any code that has been implanted in them, like a computer waiting for the right password. But as human beings, they are completely useless.

They have no future or hope, because they can't reeducate themselves, and won't reeducate themselves, or accept a version of reality that is not their own, that doesn't conform with the agenda for the masses.

They are so obsessed with the idea of being validated and accepted by others, that they turn into psychological prostitutes in less than a second, and sell all of their values in exchange for anything. They are the perfect slave!

Chapter 10: The Self-Deception.

Even if you succeed in changing a person for their own good, and they can see the positive results of that, how long do you think they will keep themselves in the right path, before they return to their old self, simply because they feel alienated in this new self?

When a person has seen the positive effects of a new behavior, in comparison to the negative effects of old behaviors, but goes back to old habits, because she doesn't want to be discriminated or alienated, there is nothing you can do anymore.

That is the ultimate frontier of sanity. For the one who, knowing he sleeps, refuses to awaken, is dead already.

Awareness then remains something unattainable, for the one claims that he wants to be free from these chains but refuses to awaken.

He protests that wants to be free, like a bird in a cage, but when you open the door of the cage, he refuses to fly away, because he is afraid of freedom.

The attachments formed around what others fear and want, as well as to a need for validation and social assimilation, then holds them with chains of emotional patterns that disrupt the flow of energy in the mind, sabotage conclusions and downgrade the potential to dream and move forward.

It is like living a life of a slave with brain implants that you don't even know to have. Implants that deny you the real world behind the illusions put before your eyes.

Such implants are structures of thought that pass between individuals, making sure that the brainwashed contaminate the non-brainwashed, in order to succumb both groups to the same ideal.

You may not see this, but you die every day a little more, to then be reborn within a system that was artificially constructed for you.

Removing yourself from such a prison, is then to deny the unnatural, perceived by many as natural, and become unnatural yourself.

It can be very scary, but the only way you will ever create miracles.

The ones who are stopped in their transition from awareness to the application of their energies, through potential, opportunity and creativity, may not be able to do it if their overall health condition and habits are poor, or if they are afraid to fail.

Therefore, one must maintain a healthy energy within his body, through exercise and a good diet, that allows to then direct the vital energy, when aligned with a purpose. But also, not be so afraid to fail that such energy is wasted.

Chapter 11: The Transition From Awareness to Power.

Quite often, those who are afraid to fail, do fail, because they seek for reasons to fail more than they see for ways to succeed.

They make poor decisions that lead them to failure, and are too demotivated to overcome challenges. And, if the amount of failure and deception is overwhelming, when compared to the motivation the individual possesses, that's when he will give up.

The two elements are relative to one another.

The highly motivated person may overcome more barriers than the one who is not properly motivated. Reason why, knowing what motivates us, is an equally important part of the process of becoming successful.

If money is the only thing that motivates a person, then he will easily demotivate, because you can't make money without first experiencing not having money, or even losing money.

It is the poor who gets angry when he loses money. For the very rich, money is just energy. He doesn't want to lose it, but his focus is in acquiring, not accumulating, saving and hoarding money.

When the entrepreneur is able to hire employees, he understands this concept better, because his investment is now in the energy of others. He is paying them to get more money.

For the workers, the salary is their goal, but for the entrepreneur, the production of the workers is the goal. The more the workers do, the more he earns, and the more he can invest again, namely, by maintaining their job, increasing their salary, and hiring more people.

This cycle of energy then motivates him to do more and accomplish more. But still, it is not the money that motivates him. It is the pleasure of controlling the flow of energy and doing what he is passionate about. For money buys...

- **Time** — When invested in the employees;

- **Opportunities** — When invested in profitable ideas;

- **Health** — When invested in ourselves and our well-being;

- **Happiness** — When invested in balancing our lifestyle accordingly;

- **Love** — When invested in the people we want in our life.

The application of these principles can only fail, when we can't learn from our mistakes and develop new ideas from such experiences.

Schools are part of a system that does not want independent thinkers and philosophers, and much less entrepreneurs. That is why students are told to obey and memorize instead.

If they knew how to think, they could reach the levels of potential and power that would turn them into unpredictable human beings. And that is something that scares those that are in the top of the food chain.

Nobody who has power, wants to lose such power. Therefore, the lower stages of this ladder, are blocked to those who want to develop themselves and achieve the same.

The blocking occurs in every single one of the levels described:

- **Knowledge:** Most of the school books are full of lies;

- **Awareness:** If the knowledge isn't true, awareness doesn't occur;

- **Potential:** Even if a student acquires potential, he is not given any opportunity, reason why so many college graduates struggle to find a job;

- **Opportunity:** If the opportunity comes, it is always aligned with the system and not with something out of it, such as the opportunity to do something new. Even the most unique ideas, when investigated, will show this. As an example, we have social media, which is used by mega corporations to investigate consumer habits, and by secret agencies for espionage;

- **Creativity:** After years of indoctrination in a classroom, creativity is dead. Then, even the most bright, when given an opportunity, have no idea of what to do with it, because they lack imagination;

- **Inspiration:** If there is no creativity, there is no inspiration;

- **Ideas:** Without creativity and inspiration, ideas are blocked by the mind;

- **Truthfulness:** As the mind of such individual is blocked, he can't differentiate truth from lie. For him, what others do is what he understands as truth. Most of such individuals are even atheist, because they can only perceive the physical world.

The vast masses, due to the reasons presented above, will never achieve any form of power. They will never become influential.

The only way to develop such skills, beyond the constrictions and manipulations of the educational system, is through art. Reason why even art is seen as the least important school topic.

Chapter 12: Truthfulness and Power.

Power depends on the understanding of ideas and truthfulness, which emerge from inspiration and creativity.

If a person is not in love for his job and working hard in it, he won't feel inspired, or want to be creative. As such, ideas will not come to him.

As a matter of fact, you can only stop chaos through concentrated energy. If you can focus on one thing only within the spectrum of your reality, you can stop the chaos that surrounds it.

The ability to attract that which you want, is found relative to your capacity to choose and remain concentrated in that choice, even if it's a dream. Once that occurs, ideas will be aligned with the process and come to you more abundantly.

One of the things that people don't understand about me as an author, for example, is that I possess a hundred times more knowledge than that which I have exposed in my books.

They can't even believe I have written so many books and so fast.

So how can they understand that I know more than what I say?

Quite typically, everyone that tries to investigate my past, to know the reason behind what I know, or even the societies and groups I am associated with, ends more confused. Because there is nothing there. My past says zero about who I am. It may reveal much about my thinking but not much about my knowledge.

What I actually do consists of applying a principle of physics that contradicts what people are told to believe.

People always assume first before they make conclusions. They are obsessed with the idea of knowing first, before they can prove themselves.

That is how school taught them to think, and they can't get out of it, they can't let go of this thought process. As such, they keep their life moving in circles, within thought processes, because that is how they were taught to live and think.

What I do, consists on decentralizing my thoughts from my head and instead direct them with my attention into the future. I do not think about what I want; I simply decide, and I put my attention there, in that decision.

By decentralizing my attention from my ego, my brain, and my thoughts, and into the future, I am able to attract the resources from the invisible world, and into the visible world.

If I decide that I want to write a book, either it is fiction or non-fiction, I first visualize it in my mind and then work towards searching for the knowledge that can help me get there, either it is a research formed from the conclusion of many scientific papers, or simply ideas.

The real world will eventually come to my aid, and that's where the central part of the steps I outlined before come to place. Because I will then attract the opportunities, creativity, inspiration and ideas, from people I meet, and that will match exactly what I am writing.

When I wrote this book for the first time, I already had an abundance of knowledge on this topic, but I wanted the book to be more organic and feel more real. I did not want it to contain only the resulting product of my researches. And so, I put efforts to meet rich people. But I only knew a few.

However, I met a girl that was starting a business with a few partners. By helping her, and going with her to the business meetings, to give her advice on what to do, I ended up meeting billionaires from many countries and continents, most of which would always invite us for dinner to talk with me.

Apparently, they were more fascinated by having a conversation with me than the business itself.

In these conversations, I understood more about their way of thinking — I attracted the inspiration, the ideas and the truthfulness.

After this book was published, many readers, who are successful business owners, started to contact me.

The conversations I had with them, inspired me to improve the book with more editions. And once I started editing the version you have right now, again, the same thing occurred. A friend invited me to a party, where I met another billionaire.

I actually met him by accident, as I was ordering a drink.

The conversation I had with him, helped me in reinforcing even more the content presented here, with more truthfulness.

At this point, this book has more to do with power, transformation and wisdom, because the previous steps have been applied for nearly ten years.

This book is an Amazon bestseller since the moment it was published, and until now. I simply took it from the market and republished under a new title.

Chapter 13: The Bridge Between Heart and Mind.

Once you apply this knowledge, one of the things that you will realize from the chart I presented before, is that you will be operating mostly with your mind at first, but only with the heart can you come to creativity and inspiration.

It will become obvious that your strength has to come from your weaknesses and naive curiosity, or sensitivity.

The masculine in you — power, will have to merge with the feminine in you — beauty. The beast or force, will have to merge with the beauty or aesthetics.

In doing so, you will develop a stronger connection between the left and the right side of your brain — as one side is predominantly logic, and the other emotional.

This is why Christ has said that, "unless you change and become like little children, you will never enter the kingdom of heaven" (Matthew 18:3).

As you merge emotions with logic, the structure and the energy become one — you enter the kingdom of heaven, which is found in the 4th and 5th dimensions, and beyond.

In this merging of opposites, you also rediscover yourself, as you learn more about the world.

This is why failure is a necessary part of the process. For you will fail if you do not know yourself well enough.

You need to go through failure in jobs, relationships, business ideas, friendships and so on, before you can understand yourself.

- **When a friend betrays you, ask yourself:** Why was I keeping a friendship with that person? What kind of friends do I need to be surrounded with? What type of people should I seek?

- **If a relationship ends, ask yourself:** Why was I with that person? What attracted me to that person? What type of spouse or companion should I be with? Where will I find this person I need and want?

- **If a business fails, ask yourself:** Do I really need this or do I have better ideas to try? What do I really love to do? What type of business I will never quit doing, even if it destroyed my whole life and made me broke? What would I love to do, even if it did not make me rich?

- **If you are fired from your job or looking for one, ask yourself:** What would I love to do? What was I willing to offer an employee to get that job I want?

This passion that I am talking about here, this connectedness of heart and mind, is the secret behind all the successful billionaires and millionaires.

Even a modest entrepreneur can't succeed for many years, if he is not applying it. But most importantly, when you learn to keep this secret in your mind, absolutely nothing can be denied from you.

The ability to interact with the 4th and 5th dimensions, or heaven, will allow bringing forth to your existence everything that you need, to live the life you want.

Chapter 14: How Passion Attracts Love.

People are attracted to you and for many different reasons. If you can speak with passion when you go to a job interview, for example, you immediately pass ahead of any other candidate.

One of the things I was always able to do, and that even surprised the same ones who offered me the job, and not only my future colleagues, was that I was able to get jobs I wasn't supposed to have.

For example:

- A company is trying to find a psychologist for the position of Human Resources Manager, and receives over a thousand applications. I send mine, go to the interview and get the job, ahead of anyone else;

- A university is trying to get someone with a specific degree, and I send my application, which doesn't match the requirements necessary, but impresses the ones seeing it and so much, that they hire me.

I actually remember once receiving a reply from a Hong Kong University, saying that they had received thousands of applications from all over the world, but where so impressed with mine, that they wanted to offer me the job.

They couldn't for specific reasons, but told me they would take me in consideration for a future opportunity, because they were actually undecided between the one who got the job and my application.

I did get another job offer, in Shanghai, that went exactly through the same process. They had thousands of candidates — from the United States, Canada, Australia, Europe, and so on — but decided to choose me.

They said it was an investment with a high risk, but because I had impressed them tremendously.

They weren't wrong, as I was able to impress their students too, who until now, many years later, and after moving to France, the United States and England, for their Masters degree and PhD, still say I was the best teacher they ever had in their entire life.

I have tried to reveal this secret to my students and friends, but because the vast majority are brainwashed with false information, they cannot see it. They completely neglect it. But those who do believe, and apply, get what they want.

That is why one of my students became a successful business owner with one of my ideas, and another became a manager of one of the greatest companies in the world — Aliexpress, almost immediately after finishing college, and even thought she was not qualified for the position.

The challenge is very often in the application of the secret. But I have explained to my students how to do it, even though the process actually depends on the circumstance.

Quite simply, you must...

- First decide that you want to job. Because you can't fake this inner passion for the position you want;

- Then, you must search for information in regard to the company where you want to work, so that you can have something to talk about during the interview;

- Finally, you must concentrate in offering value. The less you have, the more you offer.

What do I mean by offering value?

Well, if you are not qualified, don't pretend you are, and don't act like you are. Instead, offer yourself to work for free, and then negotiate the amount of time and conditions in which you are willing to be a volunteer for the company.

Make your salary justify your own worth! Impress the boss to the extent that he will trust you and will want to keep you, and the job is yours.

Chapter 15: The Fluidity of Thought.

Every single person I have met in my life, failed when I tried to hire them to work for me, because they start by the money.

They are so obsessed with the salary, that they forget to realize they are not qualified for anything I need them to do. And I can't hire a thousand people for every single specialization I need.

The extreme simplification of tasks, that people assume they will be seeing in a job, is something that belongs in the past.

Companies now need people who have a fluid thinking and can multitask, not as in doing many things at the same time, but in being responsible for many different cycles of work. And you just don't learn that in college. But that is precisely where your passion can have an impact on the employee.

One of my students was able to find a job in a soccer team in Liverpool by applying these principles. He spent one year working for free as a translator in China. Then did some extra courses to become more helpful to the team, and when the opportunity came, he got the job.

He was so passionate with soccer, that for him to always learn something new, and make friends with the players, was a natural thing that gave him pleasure.

Remember what I said before? He built his knowledge and awareness.

As a result, his potential increases and so did the amount of opportunities.

He got hired to work in Brazil for another soccer team. And then another opportunity came, in England.

He continues to expand his knowledge, now with a much higher salary and near some of the best universities in the world. He decided to return to college for a Masters degree while still working.

This boy has a huge future ahead of him. But his colleagues, they went nowhere in life.

Now, how much do you think what I just said applies to entrepreneurs?

I have met many entrepreneurs that barely go off the ground because they can't learn on their own, they can't develop a fluidity of thought, and outsource everything.

They end up spending so much money in tasks that, quite often, are done poorly, that their business never gains any potential, much less opportunity.

They think the opportunity exists, but is actually only in their mind.

I had a friend in this situation, and after more than 10 years seeing him going in circles, I tried to help him. I said I would build an online shop for him for the same costs that he was going to pay, again, to another expert, after the first one did so many mistakes in the platform that he had to take it down. But he refused! So I blocked his contacts and ended the friendship.

It irritates me to be associated with people who are so stupid.

Does it sound cruel to you? Because, if it does, please read again the previous pages, to understand that you must know with whom you want to be associated with.

You can't be associated with morons and succeed in life.

We are all learning, but when someone wastes ten years of opportunities in ground zero, and still ridicules you for trying to help, as he did, you don't waste time explaining. You cut them off!

The people you associate with, also determine who you are. And I can assure you that, someone with a parasitic brain, that is obsessed with his own ego, and with getting money, but doesn't see the value of cooperating with someone who knows more, and is not willing to learn, is a complete waste of time.

He actually told me many times that, among all the people he knew, I was the only one who supported his idea and told him to work for it.

So what do you think it would happen if I have not done that? Probably I wouldn't even be discussing with him the possibility of designing his entire website.

I'm not an expert in web-design but I learned on my own to create any type of online shop. I became so efficient at it, that I can now create a whole business in one day.

Those who cannot see it, will never ask me to do this for them. And yet, it's so simple for me as it is unrealistic for them.

Most people have this illogical idea that they need to suffer and struggle to get something, so they make their life much more difficult than it should be.

In this story, I was the opportunity and the potential. But he did not possess the awareness. Why? Because before awareness comes knowledge.

He did not have it because he was too stupid!

Another friend of mine, a Chinese business owner. Contacted me months later, because he wanted to create a new website for one of his companies. He could have easily hired anyone in China to do it. But he trusted me the most. Because his knowledge is in such a high level, that he is aware and can see potential and opportunity.

I did not even offer myself to help him. He was the one contacting me.

Not only did he asked me to build his platform and design a new business strategy, he offered me a partnership in the business as well. It is now one of the different businesses I work with.

I have always had many business partners all my life. I started my first business when I was a college student. But all these partnerships were possible because they saw passion in me. Not competence! I never had the knowledge to do any of these businesses. I had passion only.

I learned by asking questions, observing and doing my best to be efficient.

Chapter 16: The Relationship Between Moral and Money.

I have experience in many areas but life is so short that I had to make crucial decisions. Before I turned 40 years old, I decided not to look at the money anymore and just write, edit, translate, and do whatever it takes to get the work done and out there for others to access it.

Maybe creating a religion of my own should be the next step. But I will let the world show me the opportunities, as I keep myself aware to the potential possibilities in the spectrum of my life experiences, which keep increasing. For I decided to not remain in one city too long anymore.

Every four months I move to a new city or country.

Once your mind is aligned with your heart, by doing that which you are passionate about, ideas will come more abundantly to you. You will get insights on what to look for, what you should learn and with whom you should talk with.

Your life as a whole, becomes inspired, and you are intuitively guided to a greater awareness.

All the elements of this process are enhanced — more knowledge leads you to greater transformations, and greater transformations lead you to more potential, which will lead you to more opportunities and power, and so on.

Enlightenment follows this state of mind. Contrary to what many think, it is not a linear process from A to B, but a cyclical process, from the bottom up, and then from the top down.

The energy flows through all of your chakras in a cyclical manner, and it also flows through your life in your relationship with life itself.

You become more passionate for the things you do, you attract more people to you, and as you change them, they also change you. You become them as much as their admiration for you makes them want to be as you.

Enlightenment is not an end, but rather a stage, in this case, superior to the one of the masses.

That is what enlightened means: to be a light to the world; a light among those who walk in darkness.

If you follow the steps outlined here, you will become enlightened, because you will become a light for others.

They are in the dark and you are a reference for them, to know where to go in life, what to do, and how to do it.

This brings us to the concept of moral, not as right and wrong, but effective and non-effective. because only by understanding moral as a law in the process of developing truthfulness, can you continue on developing your power as an influencer.

If you only accumulate knowledge, but cannot increase your awareness and potential, you will become arrogant.

Only by being humble and non-judgmental, can you understand moral.

It may seem like a contradiction or some paradox, to say that to be moral is not to judge. But by that, I mean not judging from your own understanding. It doesn't mean that some actions are not immoral.

In fact, you will see that even immorality comes from a lower state of awareness.

The one who murders, steals, cheats, betrays and lies, knows that what he is doing is wrong. He just doesn't perceive wrong in the same way a normal human being should.

According to American psychologist Lawrence Kohlberg, the first stage of moral development is blind egoism — the individual can only see his immediate gratification.

According to him, it is in the 6th and most upper level, that the individual sees how human fallibility and frailty are impacted by communication.

Only at the highest level of moral development can a person understand the whole theory of this book. So no wonder the masses reject my writings and only the most successful doctors, entrepreneurs and artists agree with me. They are the ones who live by this knowledge and are not just reading the books.

Chapter 17: The Relationship Between Moral and Success.

You can't be successful, as an artist, singer, business owner, or in any other field of life, if you do not see the importance of communication and moral in your interactions with others, and in particular, the people you encounter.

Nobody wants to do business with a greedy liar, as much as nobody wants to be friends with a selfish individual, or have a relationship with a cheater. You just can't create success in this way.

You can pretend to be someone you are not, but what a huge amount of effort that implies as you go upwards in your achievements. When it all collapses, it's like a house of cards coming to the ground. You build everything under stress and lose it all as soon as discovered.

Interestingly, Kohlberg placed at the 3rd stage, the ability to recognize good and bad intentions, which means that, those who are very selfish, can't even do that. And indeed, as I have seen, the most immoral are constantly being tricked and lied by others. This, because they lose the capacity for discernment.

Discernment and moral are two associated attributes.

When I say that moral is not about judgment but doesn't deny it either, I am referring here, to the fact that the one who is immoral necessarily suffer the impact of his own decisions.

- The women who cheat, always end up with men who cheat on them;

- The dishonest entrepreneur, is always being scammed by others;

- The one who makes money illegally, is eventually betrayed by his own partners.

From the standpoint of society, the criminal is in jail because he committed a crime, but from his own moral standpoint, he is in jail only because he was caught.

He lacks the necessary discernment, to realize the mistakes he did, and that led him to being caught.

A very smart person would be such a good planner that he would never be caught. On the other hand, he would be such a good planner and thinker, that he would be able to see far much more opportunities to become wealthy than risking a life in jail.

A person has to be mentally ill or retarded to a certain extent, to decide for a life of crime. The one who is moral won't. But the most moral are systematically condemned by a society that is largely mentally ill.

People discriminate the least sought and most avoided professions because they have no respect for moral. They are immoral and egoist — Kohlberg's lowest level. And yet, in doing that, they are also reflecting themselves in others.

A developed human being will be moral and respect all professionals in an equal level, because he knows that every single one of those individuals is trying to make a living honestly. They are all being moral.

The same applies when the poorest criticize the rich. Again, they are operating from the first level of moral. They cannot see that the rich had to work hard to get to where they are. Or at least, one of their ancestors did. And it was the transference of moral values that kept both the family and the family business alive.

In hating the rich, the poor keep themselves poor. Because they are looking at a random association between moral and money that does not exist from their understanding of things.

By assuming that with more money comes more immorality, they are inverting the logic of everything that I have explained here.

As a result, not only do they keep themselves in the lowest levels of morality, but also keep themselves subconsciously entrapped in thinking patterns of poverty.

It is a great solution, if you want to milk the money out of the faith of the followers of a certain religion, but a very stupid way of looking at life if you want to be successful.

Jack Ma, owner of Alibaba, did not become China's richest man by hating the rich, even when he was poor and failing in his many job applications.

He admired them, and admired their knowledge and costumes. It was by interacting with them, as an interpreter and tourist guide, that he got the ideas for his multibillion dollar business.

You need to be aware of such things, and as much as you must be aware of those who are drifting you away from this truth.

As soon as friends of mine, who were christians, started criticizing me for praising the accumulation of wealth, I took them out of my life.

You can't really be a friend when people are so very stupid. Not if you are going somewhere in life. Because they will be obsessed with stopping you.

The worse thing you can do to them is become rich and moral, because you will invalidate their whole faith and thoughts for decades. You will essentially make them realize that they were wrong all of their life, made bad decisions because they were wrong, and could have helped a lot of people, and did not, because of their dumb idea that money is bad.

They can't handle that, because it implies guilt. A guilt that they avoid at all costs, because they are predominantly selfish — the first level of Kohlberg's moral chart.

If you can accept that you are wrong, and realize the importance of wealth and moral as associated to one another, you will naturally want to become wealthy to increase your power and influence, which in this case means having the resources to help the people you love.

This is what the singer Aliaume Damala Badara Akon Thiam, known mononymously as Akon, did, when he decided to build a billion dollar company to help 600 million Africans in dealing with electricity shortage.

Chapter 18: The Relationship Between Money and Love.

How much can you do without money?

How good is your love to someone who can't pay the rent or his food?

How good is your love if you can't offer a job to someone who is unemployed?

Without money, your love is useless. And how much love do you think someone who is fighting for his survival can give you?

You see, the idea that love is separated from money, is immoral. It is widespread in the world, because a lot of people are schizophrenic enough to fall for dumb ideologies that had their own perverted intentions.

What these ideologies do, is keep in poverty those who are already poor, and turn poor those who were rich, while the ones who understand what I just told you, keep themselves on the top of the food chain and eliminate any potential competitors.

Remember that potential follows awareness. If you are not aware of what I just said, you will never obtain the potential to compete against anyone. You will never have the power to change the world.

You can complain forever that life is unfair and politicians are evil. But if you don't accumulate the power to change the world, you never will.

If you do not accumulate the power to change those who have power, your world won't change.

I write books while being fully aware that my moral, my truthfulness, my power and my wealth, are all associated in what I do. The better and more realistic my knowledge is, the more power I get as an influencer, the more wealth I attract, and as a result, the more I change the world.

This is why, whenever someone asks me if I want to be popular, I always say that I don't. I want power instead.

Power is more important than fame. Fame is for fools!

If you keep working to please the masses, you will be working downwards, to their mental state, rather than the opposite, rather than elevating yourself and pulling them to your level.

I don't care of how many people hate my books or hate me. I don't write to make them happy. And I absolutely despise all the authors who put efforts in being loved by their readers. Because they distort the truth for their own gain — the lowest moral level.

I know my value when I write, and I place my writing out there, in the highest level possible. Those who see it, become better versions of themselves. Any value as an author is then determined by theirs.

I know I am one of the best authors in the world right now, because I have made many people successful in many areas of life.

When I realize that many of my books reach the Number 1 position among the bestsellers of Amazon — which has already occurred dozens of times — or when I know that my fans are extremely wealthy, that is when I get my validation for something I already knew.

They are part of a reality confirming what I express in my books.

That doesn't mean I am not curious about those who criticize my writings. I am! But I never found a single one of them who is successful in life.

I think they are hating themselves when they hate me, because I don't express opinions. I am just a researcher.

Chapter 19: Why You Shouldn't Hate The Truth.

Many of my readers become angry and resentful, when noticing that I use the words retarded, stupid and moron with abundance in my books. But I am not, and never, stating views and using words as a personal opinion. Even if my writing is constantly fueled by emotions and perspectives.

I am fundamentally, and above anything, a researcher.

When I use these words, I am compressing and simplifying hundreds of researches in psychology, and that may not be pleasant to know, but are indeed factual, and reflect the world in which we live.

You cannot become a mature and wise adult unless you are constantly avoiding reality. The need for a constant positive thinking and a purposeful neglect of the facts that compose our world, is a quality of the most infantile.

You can't be successful in anything you want to do with your life, unless you can accept life as it is, and confront also the negative aspects of it.

It is in the confrontation with the unpleasant things of life that you become aware to the positive ones.

If you look only at the good stuff, you will eventually lose the capacity to know where the good stuff is. Good and bad becomes the same in your mind. You lose the quality of discernment, which is essential to growth, and without which you can't learn to make good decisions. You become suspicious, paranoid and afraid of any type of interactions. You then close yourself within a small community of people who are constantly validating your ego, because you become entrapped in a cycle of egotistical needs.

To step out of that state of unconsciousness, means to be a little angry sometimes.

Could it be otherwise?

Could you put your hand in the fire and not feel burned?

Could you run for one hour and not feel tired?

Could you try to debate Quantum Physics and not feel stupid at some point?

Well then, in the same way, you can't be spiritually developed and look at the world like a candy shop. That's being retarded! A moron! And you don't want to be a moron, you don't want to be stupid. So you read my books, and then you get angry, because you disagree, but fail to see that everything I say comes from an abundance of facts. All of which you can research on your own to confirm.

I don't have the patience to do that and spend my entire time explaining.

Explaining, for the one who knows, is a big waste of time. He rather spend more time seeing and experiencing that explaining. Explaining is to slowdown the approach to reality, to help others conform to theirs.

I can only be an author! I can't be responsible for the emotions the reader gets when confronted with the truth. I can only give him more and more truth, so that through that shaking and shock he is suddenly awaken, as if he was sleeping and my nightmare made him realize the difference between facts and fiction.

He was sleeping, so he didn't know the difference. I provided that difference!

The emotions are a healthy part of it. They wake you from that fantasy that was keeping you in a bed of stupidity.

Chapter 20: God and Courage.

Apart from moral, another element that must be present in your life is your relationship with God, even if it is a personal one, and not necessarily associated with a certain religion.

It is very difficult for an atheist to understand faith and hope, or even the law of attraction, because atheists are obsessed with the products of the mind, and the mind can't see that which it is not prepared to see.

I have many good friends who are atheists, and I struggle to communicate certain values with them, because they are obsessed with the material aspect of life, and which is merely the ending process of a spiritual alchemy.

This spiritual alchemy remains invisible to them, because it conflicts with their beliefs.

As such, they fail to see their opportunities as opportunities, and then close themselves in cycles of luck and chance.

They become an effect of randomness, rather that the cause over their results.

Many of them lack courage precisely for this reason. As they themselves have told me, they have had many opportunities to change their life, but did not have the courage to pursue those opportunities.

They did not have the courage because it comes from faith. Without faith you are a coward.

How can I have the courage to move to a new country, restart my life and face a complete amount of randomness and casualty, if I put in myself all the burden of the results?

As you expand the amount of your opportunities, by actually pursuing them, you will need faith in God to embrace them with courage.

That courage is then a process of moral acquisition, in which you know that, by becoming a better person, you are reaching for a Divine Idealization, and in doing so, increasing the amount of good circumstances coming your own away. And that, my friend, is the best definition of luck.

I am called lucky all the time, but my luck is determined by my relationship with God. The only reason why I seem so lucky, is because I am a servant of His will.

The two things, my power and my humility, are associated in a perfect balance. I get as much power as I lower myself to the Divine Laws.

This is why I may be perceived as an arrogant by those who actually are arrogant and see in me their own reflection.

In reality, I am humble. What others may see as arrogance is certainty. I am very sure of what I say because it comes from above, from the Source, and, obviously, because I have seen it in my life and in the life of many other people. I have observed how miracles happen and how luck is attracted to our life.

I have no doubt about what I say because I have seen it countless times. And even if I was a billionaire, or a multibillionaire, what I say would be totally irrelevant, if not emerging from a parallel between me and the lives of many other billionaires.

Chapter 21: We Are One.

We are all spiritual beings and as such, under the same laws of the physical world and the spiritual world. But everyone has to apply these laws according to his own nature and the nature of his existence.

Not many of the most highly moral and intelligent, can do what I do. And I was not born to do what they do either. And that is fine. We are not here to compete with each other but elevate one another.

The food of the farmer feeds my body and mind, the coffee of the barista boosts my energy, her smile when serving me the coffee uplifts my mood, my friends help me reorganize my thoughts and write better books, by questioning my decisions and conclusions.

The love I get from the world in general, goes through my words, and the contrary, the anger of the world, as when I need to work under the influence of such toxins, also.

My words are produced in a computer that someone had to build, using a software that someone else created. And I always write while listening to inspiring music, and quite a lot of music had to be created for me not to get bored as I work.

What about the house where I live? Someone had to decide that I was the ideal person to rent it.

Most people want to do the minimum for the maximum profit. That is why our clothes, cars, and shoes, don't last too long. That is why everything breaks easily and food has almost no nutritious value. And that is also why we often pay too much to have a roof over our head.

People want the benefits of a production and value that is not there. In their obsession for their own greed, they assume that this is logical. And that is why we live in such a retarded world, most of which with very old technology and laws.

Indeed, "in the depths of my heart I can't help being convinced that my dear fellow-men, with a few exceptions, are worthless" (Sigmund Freud, Freemason).

If it was not for a very small percentage among so many billions of humans, evolution would be found only in some dictionary as a definition of utopia.

The vast majority of the people I encounter, from different countries, can't understand that the only reason why I do what I do, and can travel the world, and enjoy a lifestyle they all envy, is because I keep going through a loving flow — a positive and constructive energy.

In essence, my purpose is to help the world become a better place and attract wealth in the process. But the masses don't believe in helping, don't want to help others, don't care about the world, and much less its future, and then want money.

Have you ever seen angry monkeys fighting for bananas? That's their mental state! But they want to understand wealth, while thinking like a monkey.

Until you can put a gorilla managing a Fortune 500 company successfully, you cannot teach a human, who thinks like a monkey, how to be rich.

Chapter 22: Positive Thinking.

Positive thinking is not about looking at the good side of things while ignoring the bad. It is about knowing how to differentiate the good from the bad, and appreciate the good. Because you always get the bad while looking for the good.

The more you live your life based on faith, love and appreciation, even and despite the anger you feel, whenever you are discriminated and disrespected — which happens too and abundantly, as soon as you start traveling as much as I do —, a bigger transformation occurs within your soul.

As you transform, many gnostic mysteries are revealed to you. You then understand the oldest and most sacred writings with a higher sense of their meaning. But you also understand better the success of others, and the authors who wrote about it.

You look at the books you had already read and you see much more than before in the same words.

Only an outer interference can stop you at this stage of blissfulness, such as when you allow the belief system of others to interfere in your decisions.

Every time I did this, because I was in love with the woman who imposed her beliefs on me, or because I did not want to disappoint someone else, my life went backwards.

If you do not want to waste years, even decades of your existence on Earth, — and you do have a short life to live, even if it's 100 years in total — you need to risk appearing arrogant, cruel and violent to others.

So many times I had people who threaten my life or felt insulted by my presence only or by my words. But I faced such situations without any sense of guilt, because I knew I had no other option.

The fools, the psychopathic, they neurotics, the pathetic morons of this world, they will never know that they are asleep. They think you are the problem for being in the Truth, and can't see themselves in their state.

It is surely hard to realize that the pursue of truth makes you lonely by default. But most people don't want the truth. They want to be lied to. They want to remain asleep. And it is when you realize such truth, that you recognize even more the importance of God in your life.

You see, without God, loneliness is very unbearable. And you do go through many moments of loneliness, if you are operating against a whole world and a mass abundance of lies.

You can try to pretend to be someone you are not, but many times people hate you because you are pretty, because you are ugly, because you are white, or black, or brown, or blond, or not blond enough, or because you are short, or because you are tall, or because your accent irritates them, or because you speak too well, or because you are too stupid, or because you are too smart.

There is no way to make everyone happy. So just be yourself and choose others according to the level of respect they give you in return.

We don't have to love everyone, but we should be able to respect anyone, including ourselves.

Chapter 23: Immortality.

Once you are fully independent in how you think and lead your life, by guiding yourself under the principles of moral and Divine Will, you will gain a sense of Immortality.

This sense of immortality comes from the power to understand the eternal mysteries of life.

At this point, you are one of the chosen ones — an enlightened being, not because someone said it, or because you belong to a certain group or cult, but because the mysteries of God have been revealed to you.

Nevertheless, when you meet one of the self-proclaimed Illuminati, they will see it too. Every member of a secret society that I encountered, was puzzled with the amount of knowledge I possess, because they assumed all their life, that their secrets had to be accumulated through a secret society. And well, their society may be secret, but the secrets of God are not secrets of secret societies. They are unveiled to those who possess the highest abilities among humans.

As a matter of fact, secret societies started as an identification of such individuals, to help them become better persons.

These groups were perverted with the idea that they could create such persons, and not merely identify them. And so, they neglected the identification process. These secret societies became clubs for narcissists seeking validation.

Rarely do you find God guided people in them, or to a great extent, in any religion these days.

God reveals His Secrets only to the ones He chooses. If an individual is not prepared, he will remain blind. He will think he knows but will know nothing. Arrogance is how God keeps the fools from knowing.

If you follow my writings and are attentive to my words, and put your focus on what I say rather than who I am, you will be an enlightened being. The rest are merely social conventions and validations of status.

You see, when I am awarded as a bestselling author, musician, entrepreneur, lecturer, or anything else in which I have received world awards, or even when I help someone get a national award, as when I made a student win a Chinese national award for public speaking, I am very proud, because it is an achievement that validates what I know, but I am not really surprised.

The surprise in this case, would have to come when someone is better than me, or gets a higher position while not being good enough for that.

You can compare it with an Olympic competition. If you are working hard every day to be the world's best, then you are proud to get a gold medal. That, however, doesn't mean you won't lose it in a split of a second to someone else, or that the wind won't blow in your face, and make you get distracted for long enough to lose to someone who may be not as good as you.

These principles are the same for everyone. But when you live life as a spiritual being, you are so in love with the process, with what you do, and who you are as a person, that everything else is secondary.

As I said to that student that won the speech competition, that's what truly matters, when winning and not winning doesn't change who you are.

It is when you do what you do because you believe in it, that you are the winner. And so, you don't do things to win, but because you want to be the best in what you do.

Chapter 24: The Development of Superhuman Abilities.

As you become more enlightened, perceptions about past lives may occur. This state then enhances your potential to learn more about things that you never studied before in this lifetime, and even learn faster than others about it.

In this level, the person can see more than just physical bodies.

The development of superhuman abilities may start occurring as well. Reason why the confluence of all these stages brings forth enlightenment, I.e., the condition of becoming as light — more aware, more able, more intuitive and more insightful.

These abilities can then lead to a higher sense of premonition, and a higher sensitivity towards the emotional nature of others, including the development of a potential for telepathic abilities and other so-called paranormal qualities.

The most common skills acquired in the last stage of development, are premonition and telepathy. But interestingly, while many adults suspect that I can read their mind and predict their future, they never believe it, simply because they're told by the media that this isn't possible.

It is the children that tend to react to my mental powers rather fast and without doubting them.

Even when I make dogs and cats run to me and stay with me, as if they knew me already, and without saying a word, their owners don't suspect anything.

There are several mental implants in people's mind, operating as filters to reality, and the evidence of this can be seen in a sentence I often hear:

— "Until someone proves it and shows me, I won't believe it."

You have to be very naive to think that the government of any country will let you know anything that goes against its policies, and may even affect it at an international level.

Besides, people fear and panic with things they can't understand, labeling higher truths as either demonic or schizophrenic. "It is a predisposition of human nature to consider an unpleasant idea untrue, and then it is easy to find arguments against it" (Sigmund Freud, Freemason).

It is very interesting when many praise a dead man named Jesus, who was crucified, but then, they themselves, keep crucifying everyone else for the same reasons — because they can't understand why anyone knows so much.

The war seen today against christianity is as significant and natural as those against paganism and catholicism once were, because humanity can't evolve based on the idea that one man is more important than another due to the belief that he walked on water, or that a book is more important than others, because they're in the hands of politically influential religions.

God has not created, translated or interpreted the Bible in the way it is presented today.

Besides, if so many versions of the Bible are available, the misinterpretations have certainly gone out of control.

The same applies to any religion confusing messages of love with instigations for war and discrimination.

There is only one Truth. In this sense, it is irrelevant to know if Christ was promoting Buddhism, or if Buddha wasn't a prophet, or if the Quran is older than Muhammad.

Maybe we shouldn't spend another two thousand years living a lie, just because we fear the truth and the darkness it reveals within us.

Eighty years ago, most people still believed the earth was flat. When will we realize that our modern way of thinking about reality is squared?

The hat used by proud college graduates, when finishing their majors, proves it already — we are being indoctrinated to think in a predetermined way about the world.

You are seen as crazy when being different. But being different is how you embrace the fullness of your identity.

Moreover, you are not really being crazy when doing that. You are just being yourself. But most people don't know what that is anymore. So they call you crazy, because they don't know they are the crazy ones.

They were placed inside a fantasy, with fake dogmas and fake values, to maintain a social order, aligned with an artificial ideal. They depend on a world they do not understand. And that's crazy!

Chapter 25: The Purpose of The Law of Attraction.

If people use the law of attraction without changing themselves, and only to get more money and consume more, the ones in power always win, because the world is designed within their illusion.

The proper use of the law of attraction must be applied to change the system, by understanding how it works, instead of merely replicating empowering techniques and tricks.

You're more than a spiritual being with the power to change reality. You are part of a world that manifests in the same amount that you give in return, don't give, or refuse to cooperate with.

This said, you are as powerful as anyone else on Earth, in both your actions and inactions. "One man is equivalent to all creation; one man is a world in miniature" (Albert Pike, Freemason).

This said, "the price of doing the same thing is far higher than the price of change" (Bill Clinton, Skulls & Bones and Bilderberg Group), for "what we have done for ourselves alone dies with us" (Albert Pike). But "being the richest man in the cemetery doesn't matter" (Steve Jobs).

As spiritual beings, we must experience life as immortals, and that's why love, creativity and helping others bring us so much and immediate joy. But we forget our spirituality and neglect our spiritual attributes, and in doing so, downgrade our own nature to fit in into the nature and thought patterns of others.

When you do that, you reduce your awareness, power, potential and uniqueness. You also neglect your possibilities, your soul purpose, your opportunities and your karma.

Karma is positive or negative, depending on what you do with your spiritual attributes.

The more you neglect your soul purpose, to chase illusions, attachments and material goals, the more negative karma you accumulate.

That doesn't mean the material goals, the attachments or the illusions are bad in themselves, but rather that these things shouldn't be placed as the reason behind all of your decisions.

Every time you do that, you risk failure and misery.

A proper application of the law of attraction, is then spiritually enlightening, which means being mentally revolutionary, experiencing a physically energizing, and ultimately uplifting, state of being, and not just in our material world, but also in our whole perception of life.

Within this dynamic, the most powerful application of this law, consists in the will to change mankind positively with our existence. Because "What we have done for others and the world remains and is immortal" (Albert Pike, Freemason).

What people in this current society don't know any more, is that reality is whatever you want it to be, even if you can only change yours.

You are whoever you want to be, and you can become whoever you wish and dream to become.

Your external reality is constantly reflecting your inner reality, and so, you can't take enough actions to change yourself until you accept to change. But you can't change the reality around you without any effort by changing your inner reality.

For the majority, the idea of changing the physical reality seems easier to apply, but they're both correlated within the same structure we call life.

If you want to change your life, you must change yourself. And in order to change yourself, you must understand that heart and mind are connected, even though we've been conditioned to use only our brain and believe that this is the center of our thoughts and actions.

The brain is just a tool of your soul, as you're not your brain and you're not inside your brain.

Chapter 26: Things They Don't Want You to Know.

If you believe that the thoughts inside your brain are only yours, then you're easily manipulated and influenced. Because your brain captures, just like a radio, frequencies related to your identity.

Most of your thoughts are perceptions or visual transferences of others' thoughts related to you.

The same applies to music, television and Wi-Fi transmissions, as the devices we use interfere with the way we think and process thought. They influence our brainwaves, affecting our mood and emotions, while also influencing our thoughts, for we think according to how we feel.

The Elite conditioned us to think with the left part of the brain, by showing us images, certain facts, and indoctrinating us to think with logic, even though within a preconceived pattern. But it is by not exercising the right part of our brain, that we decrease our innate ability to dream.

The potential of our dreams is the precursor of our will, as we can't do what we can't imagine ourselves doing first. By disconnecting us from our imagination, the elite was able to enslave mankind within the reality that they have created and destined for our existence.

At this point, if anyone wishes to become free to change in a radical form, that individual must be willing to rediscover his potential to dream and postulate an unseen reality, but also to create and control his own emotions. "Every man must find out for himself in what particular fashion he can be saved" (Sigmund Freud, Freemason).

Along this path, reading books like this one, may cause severe headaches, just like many people that talked to me in person, or heard me speaking in public presentations, claimed to feel, but these are the effects of deprogramming.

As this mental control has been assimilated as being normal, many even believe that by deprogramming them, I'm actually manipulating. Reason why "Men are not prisoners of fate, but only prisoners of their own minds" (Franklin D. Roosevelt, Freemason and member of the Loyal Order of Moose).

You must understand that, even grammar obeys specific codes designed by the elite to entrap our cognitive awareness. You can actually increase the IQ of anyone by teaching an individual to explain the words he uses in a conversation. And you'll be surprised to realize that most people, including many teachers, can't explain the meaning of about 90% of the words they use on a daily basis.

A huge abundance of misinterpretations are also found in religion, and which have emerged from the wrong translations and wrong application of words.

The truth has been hidden through a vast amount of bad interpretations, and such interpretations have kept us trapped in old dogmas that deny a real spiritual development.

Religions are corrupted, and only a prophet can now overcome the state of spiritual crystallization in which humanity finds itself. But such prophet, for opposing the masses, will be rejected, and despite the fact that "we must pass through the darkness to reach the light" (Albert Pike, Freemason).

Without prophets, people are conditioned to a hierarchy of religious beliefs that necessarily fit the social system where they find themselves.

All famous religious organizations in the world share dogma, because none is able to truly understand the codes behind their writings.

You only understand what you are programmed to know. Because before you can understand the meaning of spiritual development, or even the relationship between money and love, you must first understand the conceptualization of each word, what they mean to you, and how they interact together in your life.

Nobody on Earth, refusing one part of this equation, can properly assimilate the combination of all elements of life, or even the few in which he believes.

Chapter 27: How People Suppress Their Potential.

We have been educated to see a divided world, while parts of this division were purposely kept hidden from us, to make us believe that we can't ever understand life from a different angle. But know that "millionaires do not use astrology, billionaires do" (J.P. Morgan, Freemason).

You can't understand spirituality, if you don't understand money, and you can't understand how the mind works, if you refuse to acknowledge the spirit within, as "it is God who gives you the power to create wealth" (Deuteronomy 8:18).

Transmutation is then proportional to your emotional strength, and you should be "fortunate enough to be neither hesitant nor indecisive" (Guy de Rothschild, Bilderberg Group), because "will is the dynamic soul-force" (Albert Pike, Freemason). But your will is predetermined by the ratio between your faith and memories, meaning that "you aren't weak-willed; you are simply obeying yourself as of yesterday" (Ron Hubbard, Scientology).

Quite a lot of the causes for peoples' failures are found in the justifications they tell themselves to keep failing.

That is what makes people stupid; when they are so suppressed by their past failures, that they deny themselves seeing solutions, by blinding themselves with justifications that keep those failures below their ability of sight.

That's what unconsciousness is. But people make themselves unconscious when saying...

- "I was cheated because men always cheat";
- "I was abandoned because women are hypergamous";
- "I can't be rich because I was born poor";

- "I don't know how to start a business because I didn't study it before".

Every time you have someone rejecting an analysis, planning and discernment, through generalizations and arrogant assumptions, you are dealing with a moron who has been made mentally ill and stupid by his own failures.

If you want to become mentally healthy, you succeed; and if you want to be crazy, you allow yourself to fail.

When people give up on learning from their past mistakes and failures, and accept the routine of whatever situation they find themselves in, they are going on a downward spiral towards death.

Habits, routines and the maintenance of repetitive but static patterns, are characteristic of the insane. But quite a lot of this type of insanity is also found in science.

Those who select one part of reality while refusing the rest, are neglecting the global importance of what they choose to analyze and, in this way, condemning themselves to a never-ending cycle with unclear results that later they'll accept as the truth and use to say to others:

— "Look! There's no more truth! We've proven it scientifically!"

However, if you prove the lack of existence of something, you really prove nothing more than ignorance about it. And, "what luck for rulers that men do not think" (Adolf Hitler, Thule Society).

Exceptions to this situation come when the non-existence of something arises from facts and reasons, that clarify possible illusions and delusions on that same subject. But that's not the case of science, as scientific truths come with exceptions that don't explain the rule and can't be explained by it.

"Science says the first word on everything, and the last word on nothing" (Victor Hugo, Rosicrucian Fellowship). Reason why "an individual must rise above an avid craving for agreement from a humanoid group to get anything decent done" (Ron Hubbard, Scientology).

Chapter 28: How Powerful Can a Human Be?

In 1905, Einstein said that energy is explained by the formula $E = MC^2$; a formula that tells us that energy is the resulting combination of mass by the square of the speed of light. But the quantum physicians came with an exception that proves no rule, except the one we make for ourselves, when saying: "It's all true; they're just different levels of truth" (John Hagelin, Physicist).

They were trying to explain that we can't really conceptualize the movement of energy without first understanding consciousness, as at the "deepest sub-level of our reality, you and I are literally one" (John Hagelin, Physicist).

Only with this knowledge in hand can we then proceed in the comprehension of how to combine the different factors interfering in the perception of self, and in order to get practical results in regards to the application of will or personal energy, to obtain that which we desire.

It is also with the understanding of how to operate consciousness, that you reach the blocks that may be stopping you from achieving what you want, as nothing is as clear as it seems.

"Except our own thoughts, there is nothing absolutely in our power" (René Descartes, Rosicrucian Fellowship).

This introspection allows you to understand which factors are determining your results, for "your potentialities are a great deal better than anyone ever permitted you to believe" (Ron Hubbard, Scientology).

However, by knowing yourself, you will also gain a higher understanding of how others have been determining your results.

That sense of consciousness, not only relative to yourself or self-confidence, but also the people you know, is equally important. For "in life and in business, if you want to go fast, go alone; if you want to go far, go together" (Bill Gates, Bilderberg Group).

We can resume these beliefs by saying that, an increase of our potential, energy and quality, in terms of results, must come from this relationship between both scientific and spiritual principles.

- With Einstein, we learned that our energy depends on our movement;

- With quantum physicians, we learned that our movement is relative to consciousness;

- And with the secret societies, we learned that such consciousness is relative to our social environment, as are our own thoughts.

From the association of these principles or scientific laws, we can conclude the following:

- Our environment determines our thoughts;

- We can control those thoughts with a higher consciousness;

- A higher consciousness will then determine our movement;

- Our movement will increase our will-power or energy in a certain direction;

- Our results will come out of this direction to where the energy was channeled.

You can't really go from one reality to another, unless you first experience different quantum jumps, in which the previous gradient is always relative to the second.

Every experience you have, redirects your energy and consciousness towards the next. And so, you are the cause over your circumstances as much as you are the effect of them.

It is not really what you see that determines your future, but rather how you see it.

If you disregard you present condition, you automatically gather more energy that can be channeled to change your future.

- What type of emotions could stop us from doing that? Guilt and fear;

- What type of emotions could help us in changing our life? Courage and happiness.

Einstein, quantum physicians and religious leaders, are all correct if we look at what they said from different angles of analysis.

This is why Jesus said (In The Gospel of the Twelve):

— "The truth is revealed according to your ability to understand and assimilate it.

The one truth is revealed in many perspectives, and while some see only one, others only see another; and some people see more than others, as they are allowed to see.

The truth is then to each individual as the separate understanding perceives it at that time until a higher truth is manifested to that person; and to souls who are in a position to receive higher light, more light is given to them. But if you wish to make others see the truth only as you see it, and beyond that no other, then you have no love, and without love, faith is dead. For love is the fulfillment of the law, and the law is above all human error."

Chapter 29: How Fast Can You Change?

There is no limit to the amount of energy that a human can use, being the only rule none to some amount, as we are either dead or alive. But how alive can a person be?

When you're very happy and in love with someone, or with some activity, as opposite to feeling depressed and sad, in which you feel like doing nothing, your energy level is clearly higher.

We know that happiness increases energy, but "if a person thinks he can be happy without making those around him happy, he's crazy" (Ron Hubbard, Scientology).

"We have all the light we need; we just need to put it in practice (Albert Pike, Freemason). And by helping others, the power of a group multiplies individual potential.

Unus pro omnibus, omnes pro uno, or "one for all and all for one (Freemasons Motto), instead of competition and selfishness, must guide our attitudes in life and with others, because "united we stand, divided we fall" (Aesop, Greek slave and author).

"When the Great Creator breathed into man the breath of life, He included a number of strengths and a great many weaknesses; one of the strengths He imparted to man was the ability to comprehend that in union there is strength" (Norman Buecker, Freemason).

However, people will abandon you, as if you weren't part of their world anymore, if they intimately oppose your transformations or did not trust your potential. So you must "not pay attention to the fact that the entire world is continuously chasing pleasures while only a few ascend to the Creator" (Rosh Hashanah, In The Talmud).

These few build your strength, and "you can use very light energy to accomplish enormous things. It's only with a very heavy energy that you can't accomplish a doggone thing" (Ron Hubbard, Scientology).

As you change, your social environment changes with you, and you will, as a result, attract those who match your new values, ideals and aspirations.

Time and space are affected by consciousness and energy. This "consciousness is the ground of all being" (Amit Goswami, Quantum Physicist).

"We exist in a multiverse of universes" (Michio Kaku, Physicist). "There's no reason to suspect that our universe may not be one of many, a single bubble in a huge bubble bath of other universes" (Brian Greene, Physicist).

This is why "time is an illusion" (Albert Einstein, Physicist) as "each one of us receives the truth and expresses it from within, that is to say, according to one's own circumstances" (Pope Francis, Jesuit Order). For "everybody is a genius, but if you judge a fish by its ability to climb a tree, it will live its whole life believing that it is stupid" (Albert Einstein, Physicist).

If the 'mass' we put into life's energy consists in an action that goes against our world, against our own mind, but is aligned with our spiritual nature, we change our personal reality beyond our expectations, and beyond the expectations of those around us, as if we were crossing between worlds. For we attract a new reality as much as we push ourselves to accept it.

The most efficient action in life is a leap of faith, a total belief in the truth within. "Those that have seen the boundary between the real and unreal, have acquired all knowledge" (Bhagavad Gita 5:11).

Chapter 30: The Relationship Between Action and Consciousness.

Taking into consideration the formula of Einstein on energy, we know today that it can only be increased if you put more mass and speed into it. Which in other words means that, by taking action on what you want, and with the right attitude, you can increase your energy and change your reality much faster.

The amount of time needed to change reality is then relative to the capability of the individual to accept change.

This is why we tend to believe that our actions determine our results, even though there isn't a direct connection between the two elements, but rather indirect.

It is more correct to say that our actions determine our awareness about the truth and the possibilities that such personal truth encompasses, as with this expansion of consciousness, we alter the manifestation of our existence, and towards a new reality that better suits our new inner perceptions.

"All our knowledge is the offspring of our perceptions" (Leonardo Da Vinci, Rosicrucian Fellowship).

Those perceptions have a direct relationship with God, and quite often, "God desires, man dreams, and work is done" (Fernando Pessoa, Rosicrucian Fellowship). For our consciousness is like a compass, the mind is as a rock and the spirit is the mason of reality, and through which the spiritual forces interact to inspire us.

An expanded sphere of action will naturally increase our potential for success, because our consciousness is also shaped through different life experiences.

The more you do, the more you can see, because "the degree of simplicity is proportional to the degree of confront; knowledge is observation and is given to those who would look" (Ron Hubbard, Scientology). Therefore, "do not neglect your gift. Use it and you will prosper" (Timothy 4:14).

Doing leads to knowing, so if you want to dramatically change your results, you must be willing to abandon the comfort of the life you currently have.

Remember that "ordinary morality is only for ordinary people" (Aleister Crowley, Grandmaster of the Ordo Templi Orientis and member of the United Order of the Golden Cross).

This ordinary morality is not separated from the body of energy. People with a high mass, walk slowly and make public sits feel like they were heated in an oven, while individuals with light mass, or more spiritual, walk as lightly and fast as unperceived ghosts, and eat much less than the common human.

There are also attitudes and habits that help decrease the mass of our body, and they include both physical and mental practices and habits, namely, meditation, yoga, a vegetarian diet, drinking plenty of water during the day, oxygenating the body with some form of physical activity, and being in direct contact with nature, touching the ground with the feet by being barefooted, or with the whole body when laying down.

You can look around and see this, as everyone is operating at a different speed. I.e., light and energy are both relative and manifesting differently. Reason why Einstein said: "For the rest of my life I will reflect on what light is".

A higher level of energy increases speed, and we can control this light within us and apply it to increase our energy, because "if a body releases the energy in the form of radiation, its mass is decreased" (Albert Einstein, Physicist).

Once we start releasing our energy, in the form of actions, our mass decreases, because, according to quantum physicists, mass is just another name for energy.

This is why Einstein has said: "A man sits with a pretty girl for an hour, it seems like a minute. He sits on a hot stove for a minute, and it's longer than any hour. That's relativity".

Chapter 31: The Perception of Failure.

People that do sports tend to feel 'lighter' and more 'energetic' as both literally increase in them, and just like people that are too afraid to change themselves, or even move their bodies, tend to become heavier, by literally consuming more energy in the form of foods high in carbohydrates and by accumulating persistent thoughts rooted in the past.

The Elite knows this, reason why an attack on consciousness has been pushed through the promotion of shopping malls, fast-foods (nearly all composed of meat and sugar) and the idea that sunshine is bad or that nature is dangerous. But the Elite has always done this. "The liberty of the individual is no gift of civilization. It was greatest before there was any civilization" (Sigmund Freud, Freemason).

We must be aware of ourselves with what we do, because by accepting what we should refuse, we decrease consciousness.

Only "those that combine action with meditation, cross the sea of death to the land of immortality" (Upanishads, 4:23).

In the same way, when looking at our past, and to what he didn't have before and now do, we can realize that we have achieved that which was of a higher meaning, while leaving behind and quitting what didn't seem to match our personal beliefs.

We have definitely created our present situation based on past beliefs, even if our ignorance and fears led us to misery.

What would then happen if we had no doubts but the confidence of a wise individual?

Most likely, we would achieve greatness, just as Julius Caesar, who said: "I came, I saw, I conquered".

These were the words of a man without doubts on what he wanted. For he knew that intentions are powerful and have always determined the character of leaders.

The more you focus on something you want with action, the more likely you are to get it. And yet, "Full responsibility is not fault; it is recognition of being cause" (Ron Hubbard, Scientology).

The difference is in how we look at the past, as the supreme test for a person "is not only making things go right, but carrying on after they haven't" (Ron Hubbard, Scientology).

Donald Trump understood this, when he said while pointing at a beggar:

— "That man is richer than me by 900 million dollars, because at least he has no debt".

And so did Victor Hugo (Rosicrucian Fellowship), when he said:

— "An intelligent hell would be better than a stupid paradise".

It is better to be aware of the reasons for your failures, even if you do fail, than it is to put your attention in those failures.

Focusing your attention in acquiring wealth while visualizing it, combined with actions related to having it, such as recognizing what we need to learn about it, and despite our present condition, attracts wealth. So, "Press on! A better fate awaits thee" (Victor Hugo, Rosicrucian Fellowship).

The formula is simple and has been described in many ancient books, but most people can't see it because they lack faith. But "If you sinful people know how to give good gifts to your children, how much more will your heavenly Father give good gifts to those who ask him" (Matthew 7:11).

Chapter 32: Faith.

All religions are related to the One Truth because "the substance of every object is the soul. In the soul, subject and object are one" (The Yoga of Knowledge and Action 7:31), therefore, "all visible things arise from that which is invisible" (Bhagavad Gita 6:2).

Most people can't obtain wealth because they tend to follow a mental program, telling them that they should always put energy in getting money with actions and attention on known paths to acquire wealth.

They follow what they know and what they see, and then they're surprised to fail, and blame themselves for such failure.

"A lie told often enough becomes the truth" (Vladimir Lenin, Freemason) but "illusions commend themselves to us because they save us pain and allow us to enjoy pleasure instead" (Sigmund Freud, Freemason).

On the other hand, "most people do not really want freedom, because freedom involves responsibility, and most people are frightened of responsibility" (Sigmund Freud, Freemason).

The Elite took advantage of these facts when creating paths and barriers to both suppress originality and favor equality within their system, when they created the labyrinth that life is for the masses.

Eventually, they even came to the conclusion that Communism and Socialism are more efficient to control the world than Fascism.

Despite the monstrous crimes perpetrated by the Chinese Communist Party since the time of Mao Zedong to our present days, David Rockefeller (member of the Knights of Malta, Bilderberg Group and Trilateral Comission) said that "whatever the price of the Chinese Revolution, it was obviously succeeded not only in producing more efficient and dedicated administration, but also in fostering high moral and community purpose. The Social experiment in China under Chariman Mao's leadership is one of the most important and successful in human history".

As with Chinese history, many bright individuals of our time, that oppose the mainstream agenda, are either ridiculed by the big portions of the already brainwashed masses, or face a similar fate.

As H. G. Wells (Freemason) said, "Countless people will hate the new world order and will die protesting against it."

Such world can't allow the interference of God for obvious reasons, and this is why universities openly promote atheism and ridicule religious faiths.

In between, we have business ideas that promote or support the same system in different ways, namely in the field of art, just like we have scientists and doctors challenging scientific dogmas and ending up either fired, murdered or with revoked licenses. "And yet no war has been declared, no borders have been crossed by marching troops, no missiles have been fired" (John F. Kennedy, member of the Knights of Columbus).

The war has begun, we just haven't seen it, because it is a psychological and spiritual war. "And there is very grave danger that an announced need for increased security will be seized upon by those anxious to expand its meaning to the very limits of official censorship and concealment" (John F. Kennedy).

Chapter 33: The Predisposition For Failure.

The difficulty in succeeding in life, isn't as much related to the rules imposed by those at the top, as it is related to how the majority of the society has learned to accept those rules. For "an ignorant people is the blind instrument of its own destruction" (Simón Bolívar, Freemason).

In looking at such predisposition, it is an illusion to think that a person can succeed, when following the same principles, by merely working harder, accumulating more jobs or obtaining a higher salary.

In fact, "work ends up dehumanizing people" (Pope Francis, Jesuit Order).

The world is designed within well arranged paradigms, and "there is only one way you will ever have a future: make one!" (Ron Hubbard, Scientology). But many can't, because they soon realize those paradigms are like walls in a social prison, which we see when facing ridicule and rejection.

The greatest prison that people live in is the fear of what other people think. And so, the only way to quickly succeed and stand above common agreements, consists in following an independent idea. "You can't build a reputation on what you are going to do" (Henry Ford, Loyal Order of Moose).

In order to do that, you need courage.

"Courage could be summed up in: one, being willing to cause something, and two, going ahead to achieve the effect one has postulated against any and all odds" (Ron Hubbard, Scientology). "Do what thou wilt... the whole of the law; love is the law, love under will" (Aleister Crowley, Order of Oriental Templars).

Even Hitler (Thule Society) has said: "I can fight only for something that I love, love only what I respect, and respect only what I at least know".

In reverse, Hitler's principle states that you must know yourself to respect yourself, and only then can you love yourself, and it is with self-love that you'll gain motivation to fight for your dreams.

You must "never forget that the most powerful force on earth is love" (Nelson A. Rockefeller, Knights of Pythias).

You are your greatest project, but most people don't know who they are, because the system did an excellent job in erasing their spiritual identity. And that is how their motivation for survival, as it was naturally intended by the spirit at birth, was suppressed for life. A bird born in a cage won't know the meaning of freedom and won't runaway when his master forgets to close him inside.

The same applies to humans born in a mental prison, and the Power Elites know it.

There's an "extraordinary control over human behavior" as the human mind "contemplates itself not from within but from without" (Pavlov, Skulls & Bones), and "education is what survives when what has been learned has been forgotten" (B.F. Skinner, Skulls & Bones).

The correct word here, however, is "indoctrination", and not "education", as ideas will naturally come flowing abundantly into our mind whenever we are inspired by a dream that uplifts our heart. "A wise man will make more opportunities than he finds" (Francis Bacon, Freemason and Rosicrucian Grand Master).

"Your greatest ability is getting an idea" (Ron Hubbard, Scientology), but it's pursuing it with efforts to manifest it that will change your soul. These changes open invisible gates to a new reality in which you enter with decisions.

These gates to new realities are presented to us through opportunities, which emerge from our physical efforts. So "think thousand times before taking a decision but, after taking that decision, never turn back even if you get thousand difficulties" (Adolf Hitler, Illuminati). Because If you believe, you'll find a way. "If you act in accordance to the truth, you will know the truth, and the truth will set you free" (Jesus, In John 8:31).

Chapter 34: Why People Don't Change?

A closer look at society shows that, truly speaking, most people aren't willing to change their life. They waste energy in efforts that aren't directed to their purpose, and aren't willing to sacrifice their time, risk failure, be responsible for their results, confront their lack of knowledge, study, read and learn.

This is the real reason why they abandon their dreams.

Most of the world population, nearly 7 billion people, put their attention on television, debts and needs. They trust a world that was designed to enslave them.

As a consequence, "if you want a vision of the future, imagine a boot stamping on a human face, forever" (George Orwell, Freemason).

The majority is inactive and rejects responsibility for their fate with suppressive beliefs assimilated by themselves but predicted by the Power Elite, such as...

- "This is not for me";
- "I can't do it";
- "I didn't study it";
- "I'm not smart enough";
- "I can't go very far";
- "I was never good";
- "I never made it before";
- "Nobody in my family can do it";
- "I don't have the money to do it";
- "Nobody wants to help me";

- "Nobody supports me";

- "Nobody believes in me";

- "I'm lazy";

- "I have to work harder";

- "Maybe after a few years I can do it".

There are actually specific phrases, showing us how deeply brainwashed many individuals are, such as:

- "I'm working hard now, so that one day I might have the freedom I want";

- "I will do it one day, but for now I have other priorities";

- "I need to study this and that first, and before doing it".

Most people are so lost, that they follow the exact opposite path of what they should be doing. That's why "he who works all day, has no time to make money" (John Rockefeller, Illuminati).

The conceptualization of reality is an expression of your level of consciousness, and your identity if built out of the "is" and "isn't".

You have attracted to your life everything that you believe that "is" and while pushing away what you believe that "isn't".

Many even make considerations, based on what the law allows them or not to do. But "we can never forget that everything that Adolf Hitler did in Germany was legal and everything the Hungarian freedom fighters did in Hungary was illegal" (Martin Luther King, Jr.).

"We are ruled, though it may be difficult to imagine, by a small dynastic power structure,... controlling the financial system,... the political system, the educational system,... creating think tanks and other institutions which shape and change the course of society and modern human history" (Andrew Gavin Marshall).

That being the case, in order to rebuild your reality, you need to first understand how you are operating it, directly and indirectly, as your personality is also a result of your experiences and reinforced by them.

In other words, "if you want to live a life, get prepared for death" (Sigmund Freud, Freemason).

You need to know who you really are and how you're divided into several parts that interact between one another, while allowing such awakening to naturally eliminate what is not within your true identity.

"Freedom is the possibility of isolation. You are free if you can withdraw from people, not having to seek them out for the sake of money, company, love, glory or curiosity, none of which can thrive in silence and solitude" (Fernando Pessoa, Rosicrucian Fellowship).

Every person tends to focus more in one of the parts of the original identity, while discarding the others, which leads into having a more spiritual or material life, with more problems in one area in particular, while having success in some other.

This happens because some areas are closer to each other in their relation to our personality. And that's why, individuals that put focus in the negative manifestations of their life, tend to behave and talk with a negative attitude, while being procrastinators of their own dreams.

These individuals affect our reactions to our own reality, so we should be careful when considering their own perspectives of the world.

An advice from a negative person is a negative advice.

"The art of leadership is saying no, not saying yes. It is very easy to say yes" (Tony Blair, Freemason).

You must learn to reject negative influences, if you want to protect your own personal beliefs.

Inspiring people are accomplished, because "there is little success where there is little laughter" (Andrew Carnegie, Freemason).

Chapter 35: How to Escape Your Illusions.

Your inspiration derives from the acknowledgement that spirituality is correlated to the material world, including money.

If you wish to attract good and profitable ideas, you must understand the role of spirituality in the physical world. "If you want to succeed, you should strike out on new paths, rather than travel the worn paths of accepted success" (John D. Rockefeller, Phi Beta Kappa).

The commonly known paths are part of an illusion created for the imprisonment of the masses. For them "money is the god of our time, and Rothschild is his prophet" (Heinrich Heine, Freemason).

The masses of society are too ignorant to create something new, outside the norms. But in order succeed in creating wealth, you must go beyond those norms, by learning to control the mechanics of profit and understanding the laws of wealth, rather than focusing in merely accumulating money.

"The secret to success is to own nothing, but control everything" (Nelson Rockefeller, Council on Foreign Relations).

A supreme wisdom then consists in applying our studies and development in the fields of spirituality and life purpose.

"Wealth and Power, luxury and honor, are the waves on the ocean of the world. But God's name alone can carry you to the other side, and show you the path up the mountain" (Guru Nanak, Founder of Sikhism).

If you want to know what God intends for you and your life purpose, know that "where the heart runs, the mind chases; where God goes, the heart follows" (Allama Prabhu, Founder of Lingaytism).

God is where your happiness finds expression. But "the path of happiness is invisible to those who never meditate and who are deluded by pleasure" (Katha Upanishad).

Those who struggle in the delusional section of this material paradigm, waste their energy in trying to survive, while erroneously attributing their lack of success to individuals who have it, or to the lack of a competitive leverage. And that is only the surface, a theatre in which our soul is tested by God. For "the world is a revelation of Him, its existence a show of His. He is in His work" (Albert Pike, Freemason).

This material world is moved by energy, that God commands with vibration and light — both of which are represented in Freemasonry, in the form of two pillars. Because God is found in this combination of light and sound, and which in scientific terms, means atoms or energy and frequencies.

"Everything in life is vibration" (Albert Einstein, Physicist),

The Buddhist meditation under the syllable Om unifies a human being under God's consciousness, and that's why Buddhists don't pray or worship. "This supreme living conscience or 'mind of god', which Einstein wrote eloquently about, is cosmic music resonating throughout hyperspace" (Michio Kaku, Physicist).

This ancient wisdom of using sound to connect humans to God, is older than Buddhism or even the Ancient Egyptian religion, which also applied it.

Nearly four thousand years ago, it was written in the Vedic scriptures that "speech and breath combine to form Aum. The syllable Aum is the call to knowledge. All words come from the syllable Aum. The syllable Aum is the whole universe; Aum is the truth of the whole universe" (Chandogya Upanishad 1:1).

We must "meditate on the beautiful light of God" in order to "stimulate our thoughts" (Rig Veda 3:62), because "as human beings we have two states of consciousness: one is this world, and the other is the world beyond (Brihadaranyaka Upanishad 4:3), and "the Creator created the universe by meditating in tranquility (Chandogya Upanishad 2:23).

Even monotheistic and more recent religious societies, apparently opposing this belief, aren't actually far from it, with their description of God as "the Alpha and the Omega, the Beginning and the End... Who is and who was and who is to come" (Revelation 1:8).

Chapter 36: The Path of Purification.

Although we can understand the purpose of life, by connecting to the Supreme Conscience, we can't understand the Consciousness behind it from our manifested realm.

This isn't possible even with science, because "as physicists are made of atoms, a physicist is an attempt by an atom to understand itself" (Michio Kaku, Physicist).

We can only channel this Divine Consciousness, by developing a relationship with the Source.

This relationship isn't cultivated in the many religions of the world, because "the religion of the many must be more incorrect than that of the refined and reflective few" (Albert Pike, Freemason).

In order to be correct, a religion has to promote the understanding of life as a cycle of giving and receiving, in which we can only receive from what we produce to others.

"There's only one purpose for which a man should acquire wealth beyond the needs of his family: to help others" (Valluvar, Hinduism).

This is demonstrated when an entrepreneur is trying to find what the world needs, and more than what he wants.

This awareness is also demonstrated when you're trying to find what you can give to others, and more than what you want to do for them. Because our happiness, work, wealth and moral aren't separated.

"Happiness is not being pained in body or troubled in mind" (Thomas Jefferson, Rosicrucian Fellowship). In fact, "The Lord takes pleasure in the prosperity of his servant" (Psalms 35:27).

Giving through work also increases our self-worth and promotes a better understanding of freedom.

"An understanding of economics is a bold step forward towards total freedom in a society" (Ron Hubbard, Scientology). But "the things that are done in the name of 'economic necessity' would shame Satan. For they are done by the selfish few to deny the many" (Ron Hubbard, Scientology).

"In politics nothing is accidental. If something happens, be assured it was planned this way" (Franklin Roosevelt, Freemason).

"Men who know are secure; Men who don't know believe in luck" (Ron Hubbard, Scientology), because only "the truth will set you free" (John 8:32).

This truth is conscious purpose, and the purpose of giving is what attracts wealth.

The Power Elite grows in power, while the rest of the world keeps impoverishing, because they work as a group, a close community of very influential individuals. That is how their wealth multiplied over the centuries.

Thanks to that, "Economics easily evolved into the science of making people miserable" (Ron Hubbard, Scientology). And so, without discernment, one can't really comprehend how to form a parallel system, even if only for himself.

This discernment is made possible to apply, only when you truly understand basic concepts about yourself.

Your must know that...

- **Spirit:** Is your true self, who you are as an individual — your true identity;

- **Personality:** Is found in consciousness, or the body that experiences transmutation and shapes the identity — What you understand, know and accept, in regards to yourself;

- **Life:** The outer reflection of your inner perception of truth;

- **Mind:** The multi-sensory construct of your present existence, including influences from past lives, and the programming you've received, from education, family, and culture;

- **Experiences:** The dynamic interaction between you and the world, often filtered and determined by the mind and how the mind processes your memories;

- **Dynamic:** The constant balance and reorganization of energy, with actions, reactions, thoughts and decisions, in a direct relation with karma;

- **Energy:** What is and has always been, formed from the combination of different manifestation or frequencies;

- **Frequencies:** The combination of a Divine Force, cosmic energy, and human consciousness as a collective;

- **Divine Force:** It is love, manifested in different ways and, including, through our life purpose. Love is the foundation, the mechanism and the conductor of life;

- **Love:** A manifestation that affects consciousness and purpose. It is under spiritual law that we can become more successful, if we are aware and awaken;

- **Awakening:** The realization of the difference between the forces of life and death.

Understanding this duality in our universe, is also to discover the truth that is behind it. But "there is no short stop on the road to truth. That is the only track that you have to go all the way on. Once you have put your feet upon that road, you have to walk to its end. Otherwise, all manner of difficulties and upsets will beset you" (L. Ron Hubbard, Scientology).

The path of life is a purification of the spirit in a material world. Seeking the truth and becoming enlightened, or pure, is exactly the same thing within the interaction between the inner and outer reality.

This is why nobody can reach for the truth by simply meditating, learning or studying, or trying to understand the world and life from a physical perspective only, as the truth can only be reached through the combination of these elements mentioned.

Chapter 37: How The Truth Was Hidden.

The biggest lies of our modern world came from the founders of psychiatry, famous members of secret societies and pawns of the Power Elite, who are now "masters of popular psychology, and know better than anyone else how they will have to handle certain nations and races" (Jan Van Rijckenborgh, Lectorium Rosicrucianum).

One of such lies, tells us that we are our mind, we are what we think and, as such, our emotions are out of control because we are merely animals clinging to impulses, from which sex is the most primordial and eating is the second most important.

The lie continues, by stating that demonstrations of happiness, or mental illnesses, are the result of either the satisfaction, or suppression, of these impulses.

The deception goes as deep as the name of this science, which is a combination of two words: soul and medical healing.

Psychiatry, however, doesn't heal the soul, because it denies the existence of a soul.

"Love and work, work and love, that's all there is", said Sigmund Freud (Freemason), because the main purpose of psychiatry and psychology, among many other approved sciences of the mind, is to analyze thought and behavior, not soul.

The real intention behind the foundation of these fields of study, is the analysis of observable behaviors and the prediction of human reactions, a starting point for the application of mind control strategies and covert operations, which is a work done by both governmental and non-governmental agencies, using what is known about thinking patterns to fulfill a secret agenda.

As for what concerns the common citizen, he assumes that his thoughts come from his soul, when in fact thoughts are merely filtered manifestations of the soul — rationalized deductions and interpretations of reality.

This leads people to assume that logic is outside the spirit, and interdependent with what is defined as rational in scientific terms, leaving the psychiatrist with authority to redefine attitudes, influence behaviors and suppress the manifestation of conscience. But psychiatry doesn't heal, it controls, and it doesn't deal with the soul, but with the brain.

It is the ultimate weapon against spiritual conscience, when the educational system and the social structure seem to fail in producing functional slaves.

Drugs are popular among psychiatrists because there's nothing else in their procedures that can change behaviors so effectively and rapidly, and without spiritual interference.

The spirit is sensitive and resists the unnatural, reason why people end up accepting the drugs, as "when one does not have what one wants, one must want what one has" (Sigmund Freud, Freemason).

Psychiatric drugs, and the toxins they include, diminish the potential of the brain, detach the influence of the spirit over the mind, and produce a kind of zombie, a non-thinker. And this is what the Power Elite wants to do to everyone resisting their system, even if the symptom that something is terribly wrong comes in the form of a depression.

If we want to see a bunch of humans with an enslaved mentality, numb, and behaving like zombies, suppressing depression, fear and anger, we merely have to look at the results of the favorite political system of the Power Elite: Communism. And which David Rockefeller — Founder of the Trilateral Commission, the Club of Rome and the Bilderberg Group — claimed to have succeeded in "fostering high moral and community of purpose".

Chapter 38: The Path of The Heart.

Whatever you wish for your life will be first felt in your heart, which is the voice of your spirit. "The atoms of the chemical and life ethers gathered around the nuclear seed atom located in the solar plexus are shaped like prisms" (Max Heindel, Rosicrucian Fellowship).

"The heart is more powerful than the brain. The heart is about 100 thousand times stronger electrically and up to 5 thousand times stronger magnetically than the brain" (Gregg Braden). Therefore, the spirit uses the heart as a vehicle for the manifestation of emotions, which reflect what is known as spiritual awareness.

This spiritual awareness, or consciousness of self, affects the soul, which is our perception of self, the perception of our identity, related to whom we are in the physical world.

This is why an awakening changes our habits, our plans in life, our decisions and our needs. But also changes our personality, which is merely an identity built between our perception of self and the physical world.

The same applies in the inverse way, when we travel, when we meet people that change us, when we experience disappointment and frustration. As in this case, the physical world affects the perception of self, then affecting the personality as a result.

There is a correlation between the physical and spiritual worlds, but only attachment to the physical world causes emotional suffering. "We never love anyone. What we love is the idea we have of someone. It's our own concept – our own selves – that we love" (Fernando Pessoa, Rosicrucian Fellowship).

The consciousness of self is a realization of who you are, beyond who you think you are, and demands an interaction between these two elements. But this combination is often disruptive and unclear due to a social programming blocking it.

The social programming operates only in our mind, although certain chemicals in our water, food and drugs, may affect our ability to resist its influence over our perceptions.

Nevertheless, the mind is the fundamental barrier stopping us from acquiring everything we wish in life. And you don't really know what you want, until you have it and feel it.

"Were we as we should be, We wouldn't need any illusions" (Fernando Pessoa, Rosicrucian Fellowship).

A strong feeling of happiness, and a strong instinct to do what is right, will come to your life, when you are within God's purpose for you. And having it, is to be truly accomplished, as life isn't about where you want to go but rather where you are at the moment.

"We cannot command Nature except by obeying her" (Sir Francis Bacon, Rosicrucian Fellowship).

The meaning of life is beyond wealth, power and reputation. You can have it all, but only what matches your life purpose on earth really matters.

"Blessed are those who entrust their lives to no one" (Fernando Pessoa, Rosicrucian Fellowship).

Your actions will reflect back at you the meaning they represent through your heart, because God truly wishes "above all things that you prosper and be in good health, even as your soul prospers" (John 3:2), for "the poor is hated even by his neighbors but the rich has many friends" (Proverbs 14:20).

Thus, you "should remember the Lord your God, for it is He that gives the power to make wealth" (Deuteronomy 8:18). And remember to be honest with yourself and others. Be conscious of your actions and how they affect others, as well as your life, because a lie will give you momentary joy, but the truth will feed you with everlasting happiness.

Remember that, "success isn't immediate. Mistakes are needed to learn about what is useful or not. This is how purification occurs.

After many attempts towards preparing a 'good cake', exit presents itself abruptly, in a certain moment. The gnostic light takes us as students, and... by persisting in our efforts, we suddenly get an answer to that quest" (Jan Van Rijckenborgh, Lectorium Rosicrucianum).

Chapter 39: How to Move Between Parallel Realities.

When you want to attract something into your life, you first need to envision it in your mind.

The emotions attached to your vision, will then tell you if such dream is for you, and your thoughts will either help you or not, as they're related to the meaning of your vision, and influenced by the surrounding belief system, namely, friends and relatives.

This life force surrounding you, has a magnetic field that has been influencing your reality, so you won't be able to change it without an emotional turmoil and challenges in the physical world, most of them in the form of difficult life decisions.

"When someone searching for a new life, connects in a way that is progressively more pure towards his most desirable goal, reaches a moment in which a storm begins, stays and doesn't vanish. The radiations of the new magnetic field won't abandon him. They are continually around him, inside him and assume the direction of his life. Once here, we must deal with two magnetic fields" (Jan Van Rijckenborgh, Lectorium Rosicrucianum).

When your vision and emotions are in tune with each other, only your mental programming can stop the flow of energy from expanding and causing an effect that allows a portal to open for you to leap into a new world, a new theatre of life, a new temple of God.

When this happens, "the possibilities are present. Therefore, the entrance to this temple can be described as the receiving of an invitation" (Jan Van Rijckenborgh, Lectorium Rosicrucianum).

If you are able to break free from your mind programming, namely, the idea of who you think you are, and who you think you must be, or can become, your soul expands in power.

"The material sphere is the field of life of the personality", so you should "deepen your insight as much as possible, in order that you may thoroughly realize why the dialectical hierarchy is engaged in the execution of their scheme for developing a world-wide theocratic fascism" (Jan Van Rijckenborgh, Lectorium Rosicrucianum).

Your awareness, of what and who is suppressing the manifestation of your true self, is the first barrier to overcome, before the magnetic storm in your reality opens a new portal of possibilities and your level of confidence determines the possibility or not of an entrance.

This "self-confidence is itself self-determinism. It is one's belief in one's ability to determine his own causes.

There is but one security and that is the security of self-confidence" (L. Ron Hubbard, Founder of Scientology).

We are programmed to succeed from birth, but we deprogram ourselves with beliefs. However, our spirit remains connected to the field of energy that penetrates visible things, always was and will be, and that is why we can bring forth into our reality and manifest everything we dream.

"All entities living in the material sphere and, consequently, making use of a material body, generate earthly light force, which means that they transform the ethers which they themselves receive from the cosmic regions surrounding us" (Jan Van Rijckenborgh, Lectorium Rosicrucianum).

Chapter 40: The Challenges of Transfiguration.

God, or the Supreme Conscience, needs to know your heart, and in order to do this, He puts challenges in your magnetic field of energy, to see how you react to them and prove yourself worthy of accomplishing the alchemical transmutation of your reality.

These challenges allow a better understanding of your spiritual nature, as a student of life, "for the purpose of gnosis is to lead its pupils straight out of the 'House of Bondage' of dialectics, in the full sense of the word, and introduce them into the life order, which is of Christ" (Jan Van Rijckenborgh, Lectorium Rosicrucianum).

You were born to be what you wish, as life is only about learning and changing.

"In the Universe there are certain laws which provide regularity and are called radiation laws... The radiation laws regulate the living conditions of all entities... from which nothing and no one can escape.

Everyone must submit himself to these radiation laws, which govern the entire Universe" (Jan Van Rijckenborgh, Lectorium Rosicrucianum), and we do so, by putting "ourselves in a favorable position to the law of attraction, a receptive state where we may receive a new downpouring of the Spirit of Love and Light, and which thus brings us nearer to our adored ideal" (Max Heindel, Rosicrucian Fellowship).

During this stage, we must learn to respect those who have or know what we don't, and learn from them, knowing that they can guide our conscience.

We must be positive towards what we wish to accomplish and those we admire. For when learning to follow these laws, without arrogance, jealousy, envy or greed, we are able to travel our way and "reach the aim of the path, without any hindrance, without any obstacle" (Jan Van Rijckenborgh, Lectorium Rosicrucianum).

In order to become worthy, the spiritual law will challenge you through specific steps.

- First, you will attract those who have what you want;

- Then, you attract people that offer you opportunities to learn about it;

- And finally, you receive the desired gift according to your nature.

Along this path, "we must, above all, learn to understand in what way we can positively react to these radiations" (Jan Van Rijckenborgh, Lectorium Rosicrucianum).

This is to say, don't envy or hate those that have what you want. Respect them and love them as human beings, and learn to do it well and honestly.

When getting an offer, answer 'yes', and 'thank you', act on it, do what you need to do, to have it and achieve it. But refuse what doesn't match what you want, or you'll suffer the pain of delusion of the material world and learn this lesson the hard way.

The Supreme Conscience "issues radiations which make us walk a long, long way of experiences and which, ultimately, bring us into contact with various powers and possibilities" (Jan Van Rijckenborgh, Lectorium Rosicrucianum), that if answered and acted upon, with a loving, faithful and grateful heart, will allow a transfiguration within, making us more spiritual, and, in the material world, making it more suitable for our new and uplifted spiritual nature.

Miracles do happen, when you set yourself free from the boundaries of the delusional material world, and the sense of personality that comes with it.

It is when you dream with love and faith, while filling your needs with actions, by learning about what you lack, loving what you fear and appreciating what you have, that you reach another kingdom in this earth.

The light guides you to accept this new kingdom with faith.

Chapter 41: The Miracles of Life.

A few hundred years ago nobody believed humans could fly, but "if we all worked on the assumption that what is accepted as true is really true, there would be little hope of advance" (Orville Wright, Freemason, and one of the inventors of the first airplane).

If Henry Ford "had asked people what they wanted, they would have said 'faster horses'" (Henry Ford, Loyal Order of Moose).

Nowadays, if you ask people a similar question about flying, many will give the same type of answer, as based on the social paradigm, they will say:

— "You can only fly inside an airplane!"

That is not exactly true, as you can fly in many different ways, such as with a wingsuit, by hang gliding or paragliding. And you can even experience the freedom of flying for a few seconds, without any material attached to you, by jumping from an airplane with a parachute, jumping from a wave with a surfboard, or from mountains with a snowboard.

Parkour also appears to be an increasing trend among the newest generations, that like to jump so high and such long distances, that the activity indeed makes them feel like they can fly.

Interestingly, even though our body can sustain itself in the air by the exact same laws that put an airplane in the sky, due to social programming people tend to believe to be easier to fly inside a Boing, with hundreds of people and baggage on board, weighting an average of 333,000 Kg, than on their own. And are surprised when a Boing crashes killing the passengers, but aren't surprised when they fall on the ground after a bad calculated jump in the air.

Furthermore, most people are more willing to enter an airplane, than jump on a trampoline. And they are more terrified from bungee jumping than from spending hours at hundreds of meters above the ground.

All in all, we should seriously reconsider the human logic when applied to many other perspectives about reality and life. Because logic is just our calculated perception of the possibilities.

For example, we live in a world with Wi-Fi systems and smartphones that doesn't believe in telepathy.

We also live in a world that knows about the existence of genetically modified organisms and hybrid life forms, but doesn't believe in the possibility of the human race being created by extraterrestrials.

People easily believe in the transition of energy, image and voice, through the air, and into their laptops and smartphones, but not in the transition of thought. And they easily accept the possibility of cloning animals and humans, or transforming them genetically, and even making hybrids with different species, but refuse to accept that we ourselves may be the hybrids of two or more alien species as well.

If we truly wish to know ourselves, we must challenge our beliefs. Because those beliefs quite often stop us from seeing the obvious in front of our eyes.

Your spirit can do whatever you want it to do, because you're not your body.

The material world exists only to teach us about our spirituality, not to enslave us. The enslavement of spirits within the material world is what the Power Elite is doing by following the same laws, as they can be applied for both good and evil.

We tend to observe our body in the same way that we observe a plane or the material world around us, because, once conditioned in a certain way, the mind proceeds in analyzing other elements of reality according to the same principles. That is how the first years of school often determine the rest of our life.

Due to this detachment from our spiritual nature, we grow less wise than we should be, and can't see that, in a higher dimension of existence, we can fly with our own body, because the laws of gravity don't apply in the same way to all realities, and just like in space astronauts can fly, because the laws of the material world apply differently to the same individuals.

Besides, even though we may not have the ability to fly like the birds, they do, and we probably wouldn't wish it if they didn't exist, as we wouldn't have a reference to copy from and learn with.

It is then wise to assume that the possibilities of our world are transferable. If you can see something, you can probably have it. But how smart are we as human beings, in all our hundreds of years developing machines to sustain our body, if birds only have to open their wings?

We may be more intelligent but we are not more spiritual than any animal on Earth.

Life in itself is a miracle and miracles are everywhere, in all the representations of life, if we can learn how to see them. "The simplicity of observation is functional and will take Men from the bottom to the top" (Ron Hubbard, Scientology).

Chapter 42: Cosmic Consciousness.

Studies on human beings from other planets and non-humanoid alien races, as well as those about different religious perspectives, and the basic concept of God and angels, allow noticing a very clear pattern that keeps repeating itself. That paradigm shows us that what makes people less or more advanced is the amount of truth they live with.

"There are three questions that have always haunted human beings: who are we? Where do we come from? Where do we go?

Although the majority doesn't know the answers, there have been always those that knew and transmitted them to those that were physically, morally, intellectually and spiritually ready, that had evolved enough to use the powers associated with this knowledge for exclusively humanitarian purposes.

In this way, and everywhere, schools of mysteries were formed,... while the masses received the cult of the forces of nature, personified in gods, spirits, elves and demons" (António Monteiro, Rosicrucian Fellowship).

In this sense, an insane person is, fundamentally, someone that isn't true to himself, and lives between the reality he understands and the distorted perspective of it that he is trying to control. And the bigger this gap is, the more you can be sure to be in front of a neurotic or psychotic individual.

The knowledge of truth is the only true knowledge worth knowing, because "Men who know are secure and Men who don't know believe in luck" (Ron Hubbard, Scientology). But how much can we know, if doctors and major food corporations, with the backup of the FDA (Food and Drug Administration) keep pushing deadly drugs and foods into society, while repressing homeopathic and natural cures?

Surely this will lead the majority to either die or be dumbed down, later justifying more control over them, in which the implantable RFID (Radio Frequency Identification Microchip) is the most desirable outcome for the Power Elite, as it will guarantee slavery from birth.

"The very drugs prescribed by physicians to stabilize mental disorders, in fact are inducing pathological changes in brain chemistry and triggering suicide, manic and psychotic episodes, convulsions, violence, diabetes, pancreatic failure, metabolic diseases, and premature death" (Robert Whitaker).

"The FDA is now engaged in covering-up a scandal and an epidemic, and its own corrupt practices" (Dr. Morris Waxler, former FDA Head of Research) and "the people think the FDA is protecting them. It isn't. What the FDA is doing and what the public thinks it is doing are as different as night and day" (Dr. Ley, former Commissioner of the FDA).

Most people survive in a very unconscious level and it is scary when we look at this fact with the necessary information to analyze and evaluate it, knowledge that is being suppressed from the population, so that they don't see what is really happening.

Instead, we tend to apologize for the stupidity of others, and in doing so, willingly partner with those who brainwash them.

To a large extent, the brainwashing of the masses wouldn't even be possible, if people didn't actively participate in enforcing the paradigms they were brainwashed to accept on others.

"We laugh at sheep because sheep just follow the one in front, but we humans have out-sheeped the sheep, because at least the sheep need a sheep dog to keep them in line. Humans keep each other in line. And they do it by ridiculing or condemning anyone who commits the crime, and that's what it's become, of being different" (David Icke).

A human won't be able to wake up from a condition of psychological slavery, unless he or she is aware of the fact that the Pavlovian and Darwinian theories are helping the Power Elite in leveling the population towards being compared with laboratory rats, and within their own perception of who they are, while the ancient secrets, as well as the mystical and gnostic traditions, keep being hidden and taken from the public eye with moral persecution.

Centuries ago, people were afraid of being burned alive for reading censored books. Now they are afraid of ridicule, of being labeled crazy, or becoming crazy with the truth. And so, they deny themselves their own natural curiosity to learn, develop and grow with the mysteries of the soul.

Chapter 43: How to Perceive The Physical World.

In order to evolve into a higher, healthier and more enlightened mental state, the common qualities needed are truthfulness, spiritual sensibility and honest observation.

Spiritual evolution is a route to freedom and "freedom is for honest people. No man who is not himself honest can be free – he is his own trap" (Ron Hubbard, Scientology).

To find truth within honest observation and conduct, meditation is needed, as well as introspection, through the analysis of the desires of the heart.

"We can attune our desire bodies to any key we wish. After a time, that will become a habit" (Max Heindel, Rosicrucian Fellowship)

There are many other ways to achieve the same end, and that's the meaning of life — to explore our individuality and joy, in living what matches our level of understanding, wisdom and honesty.

Being honest with ourselves is what allows the development of who we are and our participation in this world.

This state of being, begins when you consciously admit lack of knowledge, because "the only true wisdom is in knowing you know nothing" (Socrates, Pythagorean Brotherhood). "Unless you change and become like children, you will never enter the kingdom of heaven" (Jesus in Matthew 18:3).

A wise man cultivates naivety. This naivety arises from the understanding that "to perceive the Divine Light which alone can illuminate our spiritual darkness, and to hear the voice of the silence which alone can guide us, we must cultivate our spiritual eyes and ears" (Max Heindel, Rosicrucian Fellowship).

Along this route, you become aware of the role of the reflections of the soul in the physical world, that is you.

There is an intimate, sometimes indistinguishable, and also progressive, connection between cause and effect, in both positive and negative dynamics. By following and applying the same rules, it is easy to see who is inside and outside of it, what is matching the rule or making the exception, who is intentionally confusing or misinterpreting, who is clear and knows or who is lost and doesn't. But, when what you see becomes a premonition of what later happens, that's when you know you're on the right track. Because knowing is seeing, and seeing is knowing. The two contrasts are complementary to one another.

This stage appears when we are able to perceive the oneness of all things, so "let us cultivate an attitude of optimism in all things, for all things work together for good — God is at the helm, nothing can go really wrong, and all will turn out right in God's good time" (Max Heindel, Rosicrucian Fellowship).

The idea that everything and anything can lead to the same outcome, is also in the foundation of Buddhism, as it wasn't when meditating under a tree that Buddha became enlightened, but rather where he got a vision of truth.

The two concepts are different, as he later needed to apply his vision, and see the flow of energy in movement, in order to finally accept that he was enlightened.

His biography reveals this fact, as first he was shocked with the acknowledgement of suffering, then he sought answers within his soul, by clarifying his mind with meditation, and finally interacted with the suffering people, in order to understand how what he found applies to them.

These steps were resumed by Suzuki Shōsan (Founder of Nio Zen Buddhism) in, first, "not to relieve ki, not to reduce ki and to activate ki stronger", second, "to reveal ki, nourish ki and ripen ki", and third, "to transfer ki and receive ki".

Buddha adapted to his experience and kept learning after accepting misery, namely, when realizing that eating bird droppings doesn't really help to reach enlightenment, but food, or rice, at the very least, is necessary, even if achieved by begging for it; or when realizing that having women in his group of followers wasn't necessarily bad, as the feminine energy interacts in our universe as well.

This said, if today "someone says that one will be free from all ideas and thoughts if one does not think,... this is a big error.

Those who practice like this will get sick or go crazy owing to the reduction of ki" (Suzuki Shōsan, Nio Zen Buddhism).

Chapter 44: The Sexual Energy.

We can understand why Buddha refused sex, even though nobody is completely sure that he didn't have it after leaving his wife.

He did have a lot before refusing it, which was the norm in India at that time, and not only with his wife, but also his concubines.

He even abandoned a son, when deciding to follow a spiritual life.

Chastity, in this case, as in many others, like with the Knights Templar, has an explanation that is little known by the majority. It is believed that, "if instead of wasting our substance, we live chastely and send the creative force upward for regeneration, we thereby etherealize and refine our physical bodies at the same time that we strengthen our soul bodies.

In this manner we may materially lengthen life and so increase our opportunities for soul growth and advancement upon the Path in a very marked degree" (Max Heindel, Rosicrucian Fellowship).

The ancient mystics knew that chastity allows the fundamental alchemic process of transmuting energy, from our sexual organs to the mind, in a process that in Hinduism is known as the energy of kundalini and represented by a serpent.

This dynamic has the same meaning as the tree of life in Christianity, which is a metaphor for the Cabalistic tree of life, being the serpent that protects it, a metaphor for the spinal cord.

While for most Christians, humans were expelled from paradise, because they literally ate from the tree of life, and due to the influence of a serpent, the Gnostics know that the tree of life is the human body, the serpent is the kundalini energy, which tempted humans through sexual desire, and sex was the prohibited fruit.

The paradise of this story is actually a dimension of existence outside our current visual spectrum, that we can access spiritually, when our energy is transformed, or when we die and abandon the body.

Our creativity and ideas come from that realm, and that's why "when we realize that success doesn't consist in the accumulation of wealth but in soul growth, it will be evident that continence is an important factor in the attainment of success in life" (Max Heindel, Rosicrucian Fellowship).

"A stage comes when the energy is no more directed towards the reproductive organs, but rather it moves upwards to the brain, enriching it for the paranormal and spiritual experiences" (Guru Ravindra Kumar, PhD).

In order to achieve success, we must develop intuition through the exercise and mastery of our sexual energy.

Secret societies may seem divided in regards to the meaning and practice of sex and their views on it, because while some regard chastity as the most important habit, others see the channeling of the kundalini energy through sex, as the ideal application of sexual energy.

According to Kenneth Thurston Hurst, former president of the Academy of Religion and Psychical Research, the sexual energy, when preserved and properly channeled, can be used to enhance our creative abilities in many areas.

Furthermore, whatever is the belief and application of the sexual energy within each religious society, they all understand the meaning of sex as energy, because enlightenment comes with the awareness of the energy of life within us.

It's also true that most prophets and spiritualists did have a fulfilling sexual life, although people tend to believe, due to negative perceptions on sex that they were all virgins.

This idea is part of a religious programming leading society to see sex and spirituality as different things, so that they may never become aware of their own spiritual virtues through sexual activities, and waste that energy, instead of using it to develop intuition.

"Most Hindu Godmen, avatars or saints, i.e. Shiva, Rama, Krishna, Buddha, Kabir, Raidass, Kapila, Gopi, were all married persons. Some of them wed more than once in the course of their lives.

Raja Janak was always surrounded by beautiful ladies. Pythagoras married one of his young disciples in his early sixties and had seven children by her. Mohamad had ten wives and at least two concubines, one after another.

The Islamic laws' limit of four wives per man was waived for the Prophet, according to a revelation in the Koran.

The Sikh religion had a series of ten gurus, starting from Guru Nanak Dev to Guru Gobind Singh. All of them, without exception, were married.

J. Krishnamurti, although never married officially, had Rosalind of the United States as a companion.

Lahiri Mahasaya, the guru of Swami Yoganda Paramhansa, was married and had three children.

Madame Helena Petrovna Blavatsky, founder of the Theosophical Society, first married at seventeen, then at forty-four and finally she formed a lifelong friendship with Colonel Henry Steel Olcott, the co-founder of the society.

Aleister Crowley, not only married at twenty-eight and fifty-four, but was also known to have many extramarital relations" (Guru Ravindra Kumar, PhD).

In the Gospel of Jesus's Wife, Jesus speaks of his mother, wife and a female disciple called Mary.

Secret Societies claiming affiliation with the Knights Templar, know that Jesus was married and had a child.

Some parts of the bible may suggest it as well, such as the one referring the participation in a wedding that doesn't mention the names of the married couple, leading many scholars to hypothetical suggest it as being his own marriage with Mary Magdalene, to whom alone he trusted his Church — information which has been suppressed by the Vatican for many centuries and exposed only by some, like Leonardo Da Vinci, and that is believed to be, apart from a Rosicrucian, also a member of a secret society, named the Priory of Sion, and a scholar of Jewish Mysticism.

Chapter 45: Why The Truth Remains Hidden.

Most adults suffer from difficulties in finding the truth, because social and educational conditionings have blocked their mind from accessing it.

In psychology, this process is called crystallization, and explains the inability to change over the years. But religion has a different explanation for it, and regarding such people, says: "God takes away all their light, leaving them in utter darkness, unable to see — deaf, dumb, and blind", because "they will not believe. God has sealed their hearts and their ears, and their eyes are covered" (The Cow, In The Quran).

One way or another, we are dealing with beliefs and experiences that form a personality unable to readjust when confronted with any amount of truth.

In many Secret Societies, this fact is studied and can be easily measured.

The emotional scale of Scientology, for example, is a more detailed description of the Rosicrucian chart of the four kingdoms. Both describe the spiritual evolution of man, from the stage of a person controlled by his desires, to someone determined by will and creative by nature — a free builder or a freemason.

This shows us that, while the theories of psychology have been promoted for the common man to believe in his decadent nature, and feel safe in his basic habits, members of Secret Societies went on a completely different path, and towards enlightening themselves.

The majority of the population is kept blind on purpose, because if they knew the truth, they could reshape their reality and change the world.

Instead, they believe they can't change themselves, their life, their future and, surely, the world.

It is actually amusing that, when pushed hard enough to change himself, an individual typically answers:

— "I can't change the world", As if the change in the world was a prerequisite to justify his own changes.

Thanks to the programming of the Power Elite, people now accept these limitations, saying, when confronted with the truth or this possibility:

— "This is who I am" and "I just have to work harder to change my life."

Regarding their future and the future of the world, they prefer to become passive spectators, giving the power of decision to their leaders, because "patriotism is usually stronger than class hatred and always stronger than internationalism" (George Orwell, Freemason).

The truth above all truths is an unseen spiritual war. But insanity has many different unpredictable combinations.

Psychologists label insanity under diversified categories and names but they don't really study it or try to understand it. And yet, insanity has nothing worth studying.

In today's world, to believe that an insane person can be helped by priests or psychiatrists, is like believing that a slaughter can help the dying lamb.

Only sanity can be studied and presented in one single perspective, applicable to all human beings. But while psychiatry doesn't have it, secret societies will always hide it from the general public, and religion won't be able to demonstrate it, due to its innate need to fit in into the schizophrenia of the masses.

This is why sciences and therapies that deny the existence of a spirit, while focusing on the mind, namely, psychology and psychiatry, have poor results.

These schools believe that there are many types of insanity but no truth in the world, so they blindly study insanity instead of the truth.

If we don't count patients that are healthy enough to do something for themselves, the success rate of modern therapies would very likely reach zero. Reason why nobody will ever show such statistics.

Interestingly, the use of imagination, that modern therapies seem to suppress, is actually the answer to healing.

You can heal your body by focusing on the parts that need to be healed, touching them and communicating with them. It is precisely this inner dialogue, that can be verbalized out loud, that guides your mind to heal itself or the body.

Chapter 46: How to Know Yourself.

If you want to know your spirit, you must use your imagination and realize your potential as a spiritual being.

In order to do that, you must remember your past lives, by relaxing your body and travel mentally into the future, three hundred years from now, and describe what you would like to be doing, because that is who you are.

"The distinction between past, present and future is only an illusion, however tenacious this illusion may be" (Albert Einstein).

If you open a history book, point at one date, and then describe what you would have liked to have done, that is who you were.

Imagination is the guide to your subconscious.

However, from the level that the world experiences at the moment, we would probably need at least five hundred years to understand this truth. For there are many ways to reach it but only if we can see that all paths lead us there.

Our reality is merely the resulting combination of different interacting consciousnesses agreeing on the same postulates they make for themselves.

If you can differentiate yourself from that conglomerate of beliefs, you can heal your mind and restart. "No matter how hard the past, you can always begin again" (Buddha).

The idea of a restart is for most people relative to their perception of truth. But what is truth?

- Most religious individuals would say that truth is God, but they can't explain clearly who is God, and hold a perspective of truth that is actually a religious dogma;

- A scholar would say that truth is knowledge, but can't explain contradictory theories, and holds a perspective of truth that is based on scientific dogma;

- A politician would say that truth is what people believe it to be, but can't explain why people change opinion, and holds a perspective of truth based on social dogma;

- A scientist would say that truth is in scientific research, but can't explain the exceptions of his results, and holds a perspective of truth based on personal dogma;

- And all those that are insane, will basically say that truth doesn't exist, but can't explain why they do, and hold a perspective of truth based on disbelief.

In any social group, we either find the wrong dogmas or the absence of any belief system, which means that those that are not controlled within their illusion about life have no idea of what is life.

"Men are strong so long as they represent a strong idea, they become powerless when they oppose it" (Sigmund Freud, Freemason).

If we ask them who they are, the answer will be presented within the same line of thought. They are what they were told to be. But what you recognize as being who you are, is what the system told you to be, namely, a worker, a citizen and a family member.

Your social worth is equivalent to your level of indoctrination, which we call education, so that the most wide and strong dogmas can be used for some to rule over the others, that don't have them or don't believe in them.

In the end, the good students that accepted the lies without ever rejecting them, rule society and manage corporations, where the others, that couldn't accept them, are ruled.

The world is just a theater with actors acting on their roles. Reason why most of the initiation rites of secret societies, are based on performances and tests that intend to disconnect the new members from the social programming in which they were born and raised.

These rites must exist, because humans hate what they can't explain, as the light shows the evidence of their darkness.

The more enlightened you are, the more likely you are to make many people angry, and they will always find ways to either diminish your potential with negative rumors or kill you, even if all you do is talk about love or about living a passionate life.

"For whatever reason, efforts to improve oneself, to become happier in life, can become the subject of attacks.

What, exactly, are such people trying to do to one? They are trying to reduce one downward" (Ron Hubbard, Scientology).

History is full of stories about people who were murdered for what they knew, and because most fear the knowledge of others. Such was the case of Christ, the Knights Templar, and Giordano Bruno.

Giordano Bruno was sentenced to death in 1600, for saying that the stars were distant suns surrounded by their own planets, and that these planets might foster life of their own — a philosophical position known as cosmic pluralism.

He also insisted that the universe is infinite and could have no center.

Today, this secrecy is maintained because of the same predisposition of the masses to attack that which they can't comprehend.

That is why Secret Societies have degrees within themselves, and demand a symbolically death and oaths. They do this to protect themselves.

Chapter 47: What is Fear?

Arrogance is proportional to fear and fear is relative to ignorance.

Those who are arrogant fear what others think, fear the reactions of the world around them and fear the mistakes of their own mind. But their fear blinds them to their own ignorance, over the attributes of others, the opportunities of the world, and the need to correct their own thoughts.

It is then correct to say that knowledge decreases ignorance, and as a result, fear and arrogance. For the one who knows, does not need to prove himself, is not afraid of others or the world, and is naturally humble.

Paradoxically, because the arrogant can't introspect, he can't see the humble as the opposite of his inner self. And so, he rejects the very same wisdom he seeks.

The two remain separated by a wall of illusions, that they call communication. But that communication never really happens. For the arrogant can only disagree and the intelligent can't learn from the stupid.

If we need to then dissolve the wall of illusions between the two, we have to look at their contrasts. For the humble can practice resilience and the arrogant can be humbled. But whenever they find each other, they lose their own nature a little more with the interaction. And the humble one has more to lose than the arrogant.

We can conclude that any negative energy wasted on the idiots is a waste of vital energy that can be used on those who will naturally disagree with us, to show a new or higher perspective on the same reality. And yet, those who experience higher truths, rarely disagree, because there is but one truth.

In other words, we can only grow when positioning ourselves in a situation of inferiority towards those who will not look down on us, for they are not arrogant.

Neither can we be, if we wish to learn from them.

People typically reject the need for humbleness due to their ego. And theres is something very interesting about jealousy, hypocrisy, and the overall resentment towards the manifestation of higher values in those which the arrogant consider inferior to them, and that the world is not ready to know.

All of those states of mind correspond to very low frequencies in the body that can be measured.

What those inferior and pathetic creatures are actually opposing, is not the person in front of them, but themselves.

When they oppose that which is above them, as a more noble way of living, they downgrade themselves furthermore.

They will eventually fall into apathy and then death. But not before they bring a few other people down with them. And that is what they are doing, when attacking qualities they envy — they are trying to downgrade someone of a higher nature.

You can see it in their eyes, that sickness, as if they were desperately trying to escape themselves at the same time.

Attacking the qualities of others is all that the insane can do.

It is then fair to do the same in return to them, and suppress them furthermore. But because we live in a very ignorant society, people tend to believe that we are all equal, and that we all have the same rights.

That is the most dumb thing you will ever do for your own consciousness and the consciousness of others.

As soon as you take the idea that we are all equal, and that the one who praises your qualities is equal to the moron who downgrades them, you have gained yourself an implant that will block your capacity to discern differences, and which will make you do something that later you regret, such as attacking the wrong persons and protecting the wrong people.

We are not equal and we don't have the same rights. There are those who are very dangerous to others and seriously mentally ill, and those who are uplifting the world.

As soon as those who uplift the world are confused with the ones who want to see it in flames, you have lost this game called life. You have made yourself insane by deliberate choice. And then, all you will see is chaos. Even though that chaos is a reflection of the beliefs in your own mind.

Once a people are in a state of chaos within themselves, they are as dead. At that point, anyone can control them.

That idiot that you encounter in your daily life, he or she, is just one very small element of what not having freedom means. It all starts inside your mind.

The population of the world is now willing to be enslaved because they have been downgraded to such an extent that they are unknowingly mentally ill.

They can't see the difference between freedom and slavery anymore. Because they lost that capacity for differentiation. They were forced to see everything as one and the same. And that is a success for those who wished to own them.

Chapter 48: The Fundamental Difference in Humans.

Everyone has a brainwave, a magnetic frequency associated with their personal energy.

The levels go from the most material or beta, followed by alpha and theta, to the most ethereal or delta.

The majority lives in a beta state of mind, and has been getting lower in their frequency, due to the exposure to electronic devices like smartphones, computers and iPads.

Wi-Fi exposure interferes with human frequencies, causing degenerative diseases and cancer, while also interfering with thought and creativity.

It is difficult to avoid this influence, namely, in big cities, or crowded public places, as the frequencies of the devices cross our bodies and interfere with our magnetic balance.

The increase in pollution through radio-frequency will continue to downgrade humanity even more. The higher the frequencies in the air, the more insane people will be.

The installation of 5G towers all over the world, will be the cause for more people suffering from psychosis, depression and cancer, and even death by common viruses that our immune system, now under a tremendous attack, was before able to neutralize while healing itself.

Even meditation won't produce the same results it once did, due to the constant influence of fast and disruptive frequencies from electronic devices, in what can be called magnetic pollution.

Secret Societies know that "the whole universe is vibrant with life, that each object constantly emits from itself vibratory waves which reveal its nature and presence. If it was possible to throw colored moving pictures of the desire body upon the screen and there show how this restless vehicle changes contour and color according to the emotions, even then it would not give an adequate understanding to anyone who was not capable of seeing these things himself" (Max Heindel, Rosicrucian Fellowship).

The magnetic field of our environment affects our own. But a highly spiritual individual can sense and perceive lower levels of brainwaves in social environments as well, which will make him feel tired when such magnetism interferes with his own.

That is why such people tend to avoid crowded places and prefer isolation.

The spiritual awakening, that society has been developing with the Era of Aquarius, is also related to a magnetic interference in their physical bodies. And even though not all humans have felt it, and have been suffering more with diseases of various nature, others have no choice but to change their habits, as their bodies react more aggressively to processed foods, meat consumption and other poisonous interferences in the chemical body housing the spirit. "The bodies are becoming more high-string and more sensitive to pain on account of the spirit's growing consciousness" (Max Heindel, Rosicrucian Fellowship).

For those with lower brainwaves, being inside a crowd makes them in fact feel good, because it is like being among a higher power of the same level, providing a sense of security, just like the feeling of being inside a big family. But for individuals of a higher spiritual level, this same experience represents a torture of the body and mind. Reason why happiness is both a sacrifice and a choice.

You can't be happy anymore, except through a tremendous effort to develop discernment and understand the mechanics of this spiritual war affecting every single person you know.

Since ancient times, and for thousands of years, from Mesopotamia, Babylon, Egypt and China to Europe, much was the knowledge found and developed to promote a better lifestyle and health. But, for some reason, we have abandoned this path and entered another, of emotional turmoil, physical pain and diseases.

The current degenerative lifestyle, with all of its violence, insanity and illnesses, is a consequence of our detachment from the Source of life, our most fundamental Truths.

Chapter 49: Your Spiritual DNA.

The study of auras shows that each human being has a specific frequency emanating from his body, and which can be seen by some and measured with specific devices.

Our aura changes according to different variables, and we know today that it can show how alive or near death we are, as well as our psychological state.

This aura represents the external reflection of self, in a form of energy irradiating from the core of our heart, which reflects our soul.

This soul is self, our manifesting spiritual identity, although not source. The source is our spirit, and it manifests in different souls and lifetimes.

The spirit is connected to the field of unlimited energy, of what has always been and will be — the Infinite Intelligence, God or the Matrix of Life, depending on how we choose to interpret.

We are then a product of different elements in representation:

- Our job represents our role within the system, defining who we are to others and redefining our personality, even though we are an individual that changes according to experience.

- Our identity is unique, just like our spirit, but we may manifest it differently between reincarnations, according to our career choices;

- Our spirit is the source behind the interpretation of our experiences and the one who decides, I.e., we don't have a spirit because we are that spirit.

Even though we have to live with three distinct manifestations of self — spirit, soul and personality, it is the spirit that needs to adjust itself to the reality of the planet. And so, when our personality changes to adjust to the spirit, we lose people that weren't related to our spiritual purpose. And because such people were connected to us through our social identity.

On the other hand, when our soul isn't fulfilling its life purpose, we develop depression, anxiety and illnesses.

A contradiction between spirit, soul and personality, often originating in negative karma accumulated from past-lives, or even in our present lifetime, can even lead to multiple personality disorder and other psychological disorders such as narcissism. And so, even though we bring our skills and wisdom from previous lives, and adjust them to a new existence every time we reincarnate, we constantly reinterpret our experiences according to how we choose to perceive them.

We will unblock the wisdom accumulated from past lives, and retained by our subconscious mind, if our perceptions of reality are aligned with the needs of our spirit.

The two things are relative to one another. The more we live a spiritual life, the more we become awake, and as a result, the more our life becomes spiritual, I.e., accelerated by the laws of our karma.

Our personality, our spirit, and our social identity, and more importantly, how we make money, but also our health, become then aligned and in a perfect synchronicity.

All of our past reincarnations then combine, in skills and experiences, to make us successful and wiser.

The opposite path leads to attachments and the crystallization of the personality, which dissociates the spirit from the mind. These beings, which are the vast majority of the population, become immersed in a kind of trance — they believe anything they hear and obey everything they are told to do.

Their life is a cycle of habits, dramas and repetitions that lead nowhere.

Whenever pushed out of that cycle, they resist and attack, in order to return to the same state.

They systematically impose a negative karma on themselves. And that is what being stupid means. But they don't know they are stupid. They are simply disconnected from their spirit, and dead to a great extent, because they believe to be their brain and body only.

We can then say that our beliefs condition our spiritual nature and how we live.

When people are more anxious over the material aspect of life, they are less connected to the Source or God.

This has been scientifically proven by Jose Silva mind experiments. He demonstrated that electronic impedance of the brain could be lowered to improve efficiency.

His theory stated that, at lower frequencies, the brain receives and stores more information, as it connects itself deeper into what he called "the spiritual dimension" or "Alpha Level".

At this level, Silva believed we can receive answers to both our problems and dreams for the future.

In his words, "the first step is to enter the spiritual dimension, the alpha level, and determine what your purpose in life is... How much help you get, from the higher intelligence, depends on how big your plans are, the bigger your plans are —meaning... how many people will benefit — the more you will qualify for... All programming for prosperity should be built on spiritual foundations."

The Bible refers something quite similar, when mentioning that we're made in the image of God, sharing a special link with the source of all His creation (Genesis 1:27), and also says we are supposed to learn to be like God, for we were "created to be like God in true righteousness and holiness" (Ephesians 4:24).

Chapter 50: The Source.

Buddha acknowledged the source of our spirituality, by entering into a deep state of mind, but many of his followers failed in understanding its nature, when promoting a philosophy of non-action as action.

Buddha said, "Do not dwell in the past and do not dream on the future, but concentrate the mind on the present moment".

These words represent a philosophy of acknowledgment, not a philosophy of life. So it is as much wrong to assume Buddhism as a life philosophy, as it is to assume yoga as a religion.

If action and non-action were the same thing, and Taoism is correct in this believe, then we would be on Earth by mistake, or at least without a meaning.

We must detach from the dogma of religion and recognize the misunderstandings of humans, bound to their spiritual limitations, in order to embrace the truth of God and our true spirituality.

Surely, we cannot understand God by following philosophies of non-action, while accepting distortions of truth, such as "he who is contented is rich" (Lao Tzu), because truth is unlimited, and can assume many forms within itself.

In other words, he who is contented isn't rich, otherwise a rich would always be contented. But, we can assume the intended mistranslation of ancient texts, which did happen after the Communist Cultural Revolution of China, or even before that, to promote monarchic power.

If taking into account the millions of different worlds in the entire universe, with a multitude of different beings coexisting in a reality, more or less denser than ours, such ideas show themselves incomplete, even though Taoism and Buddhism are correct in their most fundamental values.

Our life would be a mistake if we could prove ourselves higher than our existence, and that's why arrogance corrupts the spirit, while promoting demonic influence in the mind.

If we can't manifest everything we want and defeat the demons of our subconscious weaknesses and fears, or the temptations of death itself, in the form of apathy and laziness towards life, we're still on Earth for a reason. But, Buddhism, Taoism and other similar philosophies, fail in understanding such reason, when refusing the meaning of action in its physical form.

We could avoid action if non-action was active as well, but that contradicts the essential laws of our reality.

In a world below ours, we would see more suffering and wars, while in a world above, more magic and freedom.

However, for a person from Earth, freedom means traveling and having economic power, while for an angel means loving unconditionally and creating unlimited beauty in the form of art. And the same could be said about power, which on Earth is related to control, but in a heaven is related to consciousness.

Those who truly know, need not to control in order to understand themselves.

In all these worlds, there would always be a different form to express activity, as the opposite is death. But even ghosts are active in doing something, depending on their nature.

The essence of a God-like conscience is about being humble in accepting our state of being, while aspiring for a God-like wisdom with the elements of reality presented to us in all their dimensions of physical manifestation.

These dimensions include time, energy and space, and are provided to us in the form of perception. Those who know more, perceive abundantly.

When two people of similar insights or dreams meet, a void is created between them and a parallel reality is open. And, what was once a shared fantasy, becomes a common reality, in which they reborn to a new state of existential purpose.

The key to that change is perception or, in other words, the fact that there aren't coincidences between human beings, and we're all destined to meet, even though realizing it is an arbitrary choice.

There are hidden perceptions in everything happening in our life, what we choose to do and who we choose to spend time with, and they lead us to our most vital truth, which is who we truly are, our source.

When realizing them, karma is unblocked, life changes rapidly and intuition from past-lives flows naturally and gradually within our mind.

We can melt the illusion of this material world with the equivalent consciousness that empowers us. To expand in self-expression and grow in self-awareness, is then truly to understand why we aren't yet as God intended us to be.

Within this fundamental perception, we become more God-like.

Chapter 51: Spiritual Frequencies.

Our spirit manifests through self-determinism but we experience what we spiritually need and not what we really want, even though we tend to mentally want that which we think we need.

Our freewill is in essence an illusion of the material world.

There aren't failures in the manifestation of spirituality but merely experiences. And suffering comes from the need to experience limitation, as limitation is the gate to an unknown truth.

This truth can only be fully assimilated upon the experience of untruth, and that's the meaning of life.

Life, being composed of energy moving between different frequencies that lead to an infinite expression of creativity in manifestation, can be represented as an electric field with a specific spectrum of waves, or strings, interacting together.

Within this field, the two most important are the Earth and human frequencies. Both interact in an effort to evolve into a more sublime form of manifestation, and from the heaviest to the lightest, being the highest of all light itself.

If humans are not connected to the Earth's frequencies, they are more susceptible to death.

According to several scientific researches, these frequencies move from Beta to Delta waves, and are more commonly manifested by the following four:

- **Beta Brain Waves (13 to 30 cycles per second)**: Representing the most intense state of alertness — the result of a heightened mental activity;

- **Alpha Brain Waves (8 to 12 cycles per second):** Indicating a relaxed state of mind or meditative mind — it is the sate of relaxed alertness, which is good for inspiration;

- **Theta Brain Waves (4 to 8 cycles per second):** Deep meditation, associated with a life-like imagination or magical mind;

- **Delta Brain Waves (0.5 to 4 cycles per second):** Deep dreamless sleep or deep relaxation.

The levels in between are the following:

- 14 Hz and Higher - Conscious thinking;
- 13 Hz - Learning;
- 12 Hz - Mental stability;
- 11 Hz - Relaxing state;
- 10 Hz - Clarity;
- 9 Hz - Memorization;
- 8 Hz - Lucid dreaming;
- 7.5 Hz - Creative thoughts;
- 7 Hz - Inner peace;
- 6.5 Hz - Center of Theta frequency;
- 5.5 Hz - Intuition;
- 5.35 Hz - Efficiency;
- 4.9 Hz - Introspection;
- 4.0 Hz - Problem solving;

- 3.9 Hz - Inner awareness;

- 3.5 Hz - Regeneration;

- 3 Hz - Tranquility;

- 1 Hz - Harmony.

We can resume the previous list by observing these three states:

- **The Highest State of Being:** Absence of thought, with an awareness based on intuition.

- **The Medium State of Being:** Thought directed towards creativity, visualization and dreaming.

- **The Lowest State of Being:** Constant thinking, as an effect of the environment.

Chapter 52: How to Maintain a Higher Frequency?

Jose Silva found in his experiments that, once the mind quiets down, it is easier to get in touch with the Higher Intelligence.

This means that we can collect information from a conscious state of mind, as well as from a subconscious state of mind, or deeper conscious level – the Source.

This Source can be identified as God, the Holy Spirit, the energy field, or quite simply, the 4th and 5th dimensions. And so we know that our mind can operate like an antenna, connecting to, and collecting, information, emanating from different dimensions.

Here we have the explanation as to why some people are telepathic and others are able to channel spiritual beings. In both cases, they are operating from a higher state of being, a different frequency, that for the vast majority of the population is far from reach.

In this sense, the practices and rituals of the many Secret Societies, do prepare the individual to ascend to a higher state, which then allows him to collect information from different realms of existence.

In doing so, if the individual is guided by a higher moral, he will naturally attract information that uplifts the planet. And if he is guided by a lower density of thought, he will attract spiritual forms of a lower dimension.

As such, we can understand why so many people distrust this knowledge, for their ignorance is equivalent to their vibration. They have to fear that which they can't understand because they are stupid.

It is for these reasons that the information and the techniques were kept secret for thousands of years and accessible only to a few — chosen people.

The vast majority of the population is too obsessed with their own greed to deserve such information.

We are between two worlds — physical and spiritual. But the spiritual world doesn't belong to some church and prayers or chants.

This spiritual world is part of the realm of the physical. Both intersect each other within our mind.

If we cannot see this, and live accordingly, we are not spiritual. As such, we are like walking dead.

Whenever a person refuses to live with this awareness, that person is just not alive. She may be living, but she is not truly alive.

Enlightenment is then not a transcendental condition but rather a state that follows others:

- **Purpose:** The willingness to do according to who you are;

- **Realization:** When you fulfill your goals by living them;

- **Awareness:** When you understand that you are part of the spiritual world;

- **Consciousness:** When you live between two worlds;

- **Enlightenment:** When the physical and spiritual are one in your mind.

The expansion of these perceptions, obviously depends on our capacity to avoid being trapped by the emotions and thoughts produced by a physical world, composed mostly by morons, who are walking around like zombies, and have no control over their own mind and thoughts.

Our path depends on the capacity to control the effects of the emotional stimulations produced outside of us — fear, worries, anxiety and anger.

The ideal balance isn't achieved when realizing that the world is an illusion and emotions must be suppressed, but instead when you learn to accept your emotions beyond the illusion of reality, in order to assimilate a higher realm beyond the perceptions that your brain can assimilate.

It is only at that point, that the perceptions of the spiritual realm allow you to expand your awareness and reach a new state of being.

You can't do that without knowledge, and you can't become enlightened by reading garbage.

Only the knowledge of truth allows you to reach for that ideal state.

Chapter 53: Truth Has Its Own Frequency.

If you want the truth, you must find it in my books. If you read anything else, you risk going downwards in your perceptions, because most books either contain lies or misinterpretations.

You simply cannot see the truth, not until you develop discernment. But you will never develop discernment, if you keep reading information that downgrades your mind.

As you ascend, that capacity will be more easily applicable. And then, but only then, you will be able to look back, and know which books brought you there. You will be able to differentiate truth from lie.

I can do that but most people can't. And the most stupid thing they will ever do to themselves, is to think I am like them, or to compare me with them.

Most of the morons I have found in many Secret Societies, think they know me, because they compare me with themselves, with what they know. But I have surpassed all religions of Earth.

If you do not follow what I say, you waste your time. If you do, you will reach for enlightenment. And then, you will see what I see. You will be able to look at everything you read all your life and know where is truth and where is lie. You will know the difference.

Most importantly, you will know who are the people that are actively bringing humanity downwards to hell. And you will also know their tricks and tactics, because by seeing the truth, you will be able to see how they are trapping the souls on Earth.

Very few people will be able to ascend to a Higher Kingdom. But it is my goal to take as many as possible there. Even though, from what I have observed already, I am merely connecting to the chosen ones. God has already made His election.

The chosen ones are deceived because they lack knowledge. I am here to provide it.

When you read my books, you merge with the higher frequencies.

These aren't just words. As you reach for the higher frequencies, by reading my books, your mind will enter that ideal state, from where the Source connects to you.

As many of my readers have found, you are then able to communicate directly to God and even receive his answers more clearly.

Throughout history, all religions were corrupted, as unprepared souls aren't suppose to ascend spiritually and access these revelations.

God is now using individuals only to bring this Truth to the world. These chosen prophets are here to reveal this truth.

If you can see them, behind the curtain of lies of the world, you will see that they are all speaking the same. But if you confuse prophets with demons, then you will naturally feel confused about the message as well. You will not see the truth.

This supreme revelation is within everyone and we can feel it when having it, if living a spiritual life.

What the material world can do, is only present us assumptions enforced by mass belief. And it is only natural that unprepared spirits fear the truth, as it is contrary to their nature.

That truth represents their destruction from the realm of Earth, and death is feared by everyone. For many spirits seek to reincarnate as a body of flesh, even if they end up wasting their entire existence with a kind of amnesia as to why they are alive in a body.

People want to be eternal in human flesh, with a disconnection from the Source, and that has been the main purpose of those who are in Power — to connect everyone to a computer or AI.

Then, they can make themselves and their chosen ones immortal, by subverting the laws of God.

Chapter 54: The Real Spiritual Battle.

The battle between Christians and anti-Christians, or in general, between any religion and its demons, is a schizophrenic interpretation of the masses related to their extreme low level of consciousness.

In truth they are their own demons. The war is happening inside their mind.

It is a war between the ones who want to merge with machines, and those who want to ascend to higher realms, and be part of the galactic collective — the cosmic consciousness, represented by the many interplanetary families of extraterrestrials, either they look like us or not.

In this sense, both demons and angels are already here.

Prophets are the angels, and demons are the obsessed with their own egotistic needs. And yes, angels and demons merge with one another inside their own families, at work, in politics, and pretty much everywhere.

Even the fact that a large portion of the planet is xenophobic and racist, proves to you that the masses cannot ascend to that ideal state of collective awareness that I am talking about here. Because if a person rejects other humans due the color of their skin, how can this person comprehend living beings that are far more complex organically and distant from us in their DNA?

They can't! So they naturally have to be demonic!

It doesn't matter to which religious congregation they are associated, because they will simply not ascend. They must die and never reborn in a body again, or at least, not a body within this dimension.

As this planet ascends to a higher dimension, many souls will have to travel to planets of a higher density, where they will experience their own ignorance in a more dense jail — composed of a lower way of living, and guided mostly by the lowest emotions — fear of death and a strong need for survival.

The idea that we are all the same is another illusion of this world. We are not.

Some are working in one direction — to downgrade humanity, and the others are speaking in another direction — to uplift it. And while those who are downgrading souls, keep destroying the reputation and works of those who are uplifting them, the ones who are uplifting the world are often found isolated, because the broad masses are too stupid to see them.

The vast majority of the planet is infested with demons. That is why so many prophets were murdered and mocked in the past, and continue to be to these days.

As Jesus said, "if those who lead you say to you, "See, the Kingdom is in the sky", then the birds of the sky will precede you. If they say to you, "It is in the sea", then the fish will precede you. Rather, the Kingdom is inside of you, and it is outside of you.

When you come to know yourselves, then you will become known, and you will realize that it is you who are the sons of the living Father. But if you will not know yourselves, you dwell in poverty, and it is you who are that poverty" (Jesus Christ, In Gospel of Thomas — Nag Hammadi Library).

Chapter 55: The Energy of Nature.

The meaning of being enlightened is the same as being in harmony with the light of Earth — its energy and the path beyond it.

Baker (1995), as well as many other scientists, measured the frequency of several trees under different environmental conditions, to conclude that the values show numbers between 0.2 Hz and 2 Hz.

This means that a tree, in its healthier state, will have the lowest frequency a human being can ever reach. Which leads us to assume that, as mankind has been destroying its forests, for each tree that dies, the world becomes more insane.

The Native Americans were right in saying that we're one with nature. "Whatever we do to the web, we do to ourselves. All things are bound together. All things connect" (Chief Seattle).

We are part of nature and composed by its elements. "The Great Spirit is in all things, the Great Spirit is our Father, but the Earth is our Mother. She nourishes us..." (Big Thunder Bedagi Wabanaki Algonquin).

The more we connect with our Mother Earth, the more spiritual our personal frequencies become. "Man's heart away from nature becomes hard" (Standing Bear, Ponca Tribe).

This evidence can be demonstrated by several studies on animal brainwave frequencies, or EEC (Electroencephalography Studying), when compared with what is seen in human beings:

- Humans (Adults) – 14 Hz;
- Monkeys – 7-9 Hz;
- Rats - 6-10 Hz;
- Cats & Rabbits – 4-6 Hz.

This information leads us to rethink the concept of human intelligence, or the idea of human beings as superior life-forms when compared to the rest of nature.

There is no intelligence in a being that, from a high-frequency status, self-destroys himself in anger and fear. And surely, there is no intelligence in a being that refuses to cooperate with Mother Earth, in expanding his own survival, by being more natural in his habits, diet and consumption of energy.

There is a huge contradiction to this principle in the human species, which takes nature's resources for material gainings and selfish needs, while destroying the only source of energy and life.

This kind of species, in not only selfish within one generation, but also towards the future of all, as it diminishes their potential to survive on the planet.

Children born in today's world are raised with genetically modified organisms, while drinking poisonous water, breathing polluted air and being exposed to a severely radiated environment.

Even if their life expectancy isn't sabotaged by sudden diseases, like a cancer or a stroke, before they reach their 40s, their biological DNA is already being modified to such a degree that, more than being highly prone to depression and other mental disorders, they are less likely to acknowledge their spirituality or become able to develop it.

We must "respect food, for food sustains the body, and the body exists to serve the soul" (The Upanishads 4:10).

Chapter 56: How a Spiritual Life Makes You Rich.

In today's world, learning disorders may be seen as symptoms of cognitive disabilities, but they are actually symptoms of a damaged spirituality.

A child with an awaken spirituality, can learn anything. "The Soul is that which makes the mind think" (Upanishads 4:13).

Religions and sciences, promoting the idea of humans being equal to animals, while suggesting that a life, without material needs or efforts, is spiritual, also deny humans from their own spiritual path.

"Religious people, who devote themselves to rituals and sacrifices, are ignorant of their ignorance" (Upanishads 5:5).

God's purpose, when allowing human abilities that animals don't have, and making them sacred, was clearly stated, as "the end of life is to be like God, and the soul following God will be like Him" (Socrates).

The strength of our spirituality then comes from the intended cooperation in promoting life on Earth, in order to expand survival in all that unifies nature.

It is our responsibility to progress and keep developing the world, while learning with our actions, by building a reality that promotes Earth's Frequencies in their purest forms, but also life in general, wherever it grows, and no matter how it's manifested.

"The love of money is the root of all kinds of evil" (Timothy 6:10), because humans should be loving life instead.

A rich individual profiting from fulfilling activities, donating to the needed and helping mankind with his actions, has money with God's blessing, because every "selfless action is inspired by God" (Bhagavad Gita 5:16).

Jesus said that, "anyone who gives up anything for the kingdom of God, will certainly receive many times more in this life, and will receive eternal life in the next world to come" (Luke 18). "The wealth of those who give generously never runs out" (Vedas 2:1).

Our world could be very different, and we already possess the required knowledge and technology to make it possible. We could be free of pollution, destruction, wars, selfishness and fear. It is truly a choice and, throughout history, many have given their lives so that we could have it now.

Refusing to act within the meaning of life, is to accept death, in a world self-destroying itself with all life on it — not only the physical but also spiritual.

How would our planet become, if all energy was clean and machines, operated by computers, did all of men's work?

How can we create computers that put a Boing 787 in the air, but not computers that sustain life on Earth in an automatic way, while releasing us from the slavery of money?

If such things were made possible, we could have freedom to expand our creativity and live the life we want.

In such world, we would be free to dream and truly live our dreams. We would be God-like, while manifesting our true nature.

It is our self-destructive condition that impedes us from using what is already available in order to achieve such lifestyle.

In a normal world, we would be fully experiencing and expanding in our consciousness, and that would be a kind of heaven on Earth.

Many don't seem prepared to envision this possibility, and that is why we are not heading there, to that realm, as fast as we should.

Chapter 57: Human Development and Spirituality.

The brainwave frequency in human beings changes as they grow up:

- Delta – 0 to 4 years old;
- Theta – 4 to 7 years old;
- Alpha – 7 to 14 years old;
- Beta – 14 years old and more.

Can then anyone say, "I don't like children"?

For a person that doesn't love children is surely in a very distant frequency from them. And a person who hurts children is probably a demon.

The opposite shows itself in the form of a childlike frequency. "An honest man is always a child" (Socrates).

You can also more or less judge the frequency range of a group, by noticing how interactions occur, as we tend to feel good among people of a similar frequency to ours, and uncomfortable with those in a more distant reach.

Even though most would disagree with the idea of cataloging humans in levels, the truth is that they do exist, which means that, in the highest of the most positive ranges, we find individuals promoting survival in their surroundings, namely, with their friends and nature — they love animals, children and trees, and tend to express the most positive vibration.

Destructive people will show admiration and interest towards what expresses their state of mind, namely, destruction, anger, fear and death, and, generally speaking, suppressive behavior.

This differentiation can be seen, when we notice how the energy inside an environment changes people's mood towards a specific situation.

That is also how sensitive individuals develop the ability of having premonitions.

A person in a positive frequency will feel good when in contact with nature, while negative individuals feel better when dealing with anger and fear, or destruction — from a selfish, arrogant and superior perspective.

That is why psychopaths are prone to choose positions of power inside society.

The cruelest atrocities in history were committed by psychiatrists, priests, physicians, politicians, police officers, soldiers, kings and emperors.

The smile of an individual during an argument, or when seeing someone suffering, will also show you a glimpse of his demonic nature.

Most people are more willing to watch a fight or accident, than to take responsibility in stopping that, for such is the nature of most human beings.

More could be said, namely, that we should always suspect those who feel good among the dead, nearly dead or insane, as they feel related to that frequency. They feel powerful when playing a position of power over those who suffer.

This sadistic nature, whatsoever is the profession, background or knowledge one possesses, hides another deeper and darker truth, which is that death is contagious by frequency vibration.

Among the professionals with the highest number of suicides, we find:

- Psychiatrists, psychologists and physicians;
- Nurses, dentists and veterinarians;
- Medical scientists and pharmacists;
- Judges, lawyers, police officers and guards.

We should also suspect those feeling better in society than in nature, as the majority, especially in big cities, shows the worse frequencies, due to their extensive and prolonged exposure to Wi-Fi frequencies, radio frequencies and radiation in general.

Chapter 58: The Frequency of a Culture.

How can you feel good in an environment in which there is no interaction or communication between you and others, such as shopping malls or clubs, unless you are within the same frequency of what is being experienced in that same environment?

Very highly spiritual individuals never feel good among crowds. They feel drained in their energy and very exhausted.

I love to be among people, for example, but I can't.

If I am not among individuals of a good frequency, I easily start to fall asleep, because I can't handle such immense quantity of a negative range frequency.

The same I could say about certain countries and cultures. For there is a correlation between suicide, psychopathy, frequencies and cultures.

Lithuania, for example, systematically occupies the first position in the world for suicide, because they have the highest ratio of psychopaths per habitants.

They are also one of the most xenophobic and racist nations on Earth. And their universities look more like a primary school for those who come from other countries.

Their diplomas are not worth toilet paper, and yet, they praise themselves for having one of the highest ratios of college graduates in the world, while hiding the fact that nobody fails exams in Lithuania.

Any moron can have a college certificate in this country.

It is then with no surprise that the majority of the population in this country is proudly atheist, for many of them are also proudly stupid.

I have never been in such a country, where so many people know nothing but think they know everything.

This is clearly the most challenging nation for those who wish to be spiritual and creative — the highest state of mind.

It would be foolish to like such a people, no matter what kind of history they have to justify their very low state of mind. For "a friend to all, is a friend to none" (Aristotle).

The ability to differentiate what is horrible from what is ideal, is part of your development in discernment. It is healthy to hate Lithuanians and Lithuania, unless you see differences that don't justify the rule, I.e., unless you encounter exceptions.

Many would say that we can't generalize a country, but that would be like saying that a country doesn't justify itself by the amount of people who want it.

Yes, you can generalize assumptions, when a majority of a people show a certain predisposition.

That's what countries are — illusory borders encompassing a majority, or group.

For how many generations this group makes the country is irrelevant. A country is always a representation of its people. Besides that, the rest are just stories that people tell themselves to justify their decisions in life.

In truth, if you don't like where you are, you should be able to leave. And I hope one day, some government, becomes smart enough to give passports, not based on the location of its citizens but their level of contribution or willingness to be part of it. For not only can they collect more taxes by doing this, but also free people from the restrictions of an imaginary line called frontier.

If we can do this, we can change the world more rapidly. Because, even though we dare to say that nazism is part of the past, as soon as you go near the Auschwitz concentration camp, it becomes clear that nothing has ended. The racist nazis of that time, are now the habitants of the nearby city of Krakow.

The frequency is the same. The people of Krakow are extremely racist and xenophobic.

Many of them, either openly admit it or will insult you in their native language, thinking you don't understand.

It makes you wonder if they are all descendants of those who worked in these camps for the German side of the battle.

Chapter 59: Recognizing Danger and Love.

Being spiritual isn't an easy choice, and the most spiritual religious groups in history have long vanished from Earth or are now minorities, as it is the case of Gnosticism.

The choice of developing our spirituality beyond common standards, also means risking being rejected by our peers and relatives, as they won't feel connected anymore, even if not finding reasons for such behavior.

Reasons will even be created in order to justify a premeditated choice towards rejecting what doesn't match their own nature.

If, when entering a room full of people and, before any communication, you are noticed, insulted, rejected and ridiculed, know that you're closer to God than anyone else in that room.

The Bible mentions this evidence, when referring that we should "Love not the world, neither the things that are in the world.

If any man loves the world, the love of the Father is not in him. For all that is in the world, the lust of the flesh, and the lust of the eyes, and the pride of life, is not of the Father, but is of the world. And the world passes away, and the lust thereof: but he that does the will of God abides forever" (John 2:15).

When meeting a person for the first time, you can notice that the reaction will include either looking into your eyes with a smile or refusing it, while transmitting a sense of rejection.

In ancient times, wise men already knew that the eyes are the mirror of the soul. As Aristotle mentioned, "Love is composed of a single soul inhabiting two bodies".

This means that we express in our eyes what is felt in our heart.

This feeling comes from the acknowledgment of a certain distinct frequency. "At Beta we prey on each other; at Alpha we pray for one another" (Jose Silva).

People of different frequencies repel themselves, while those with similar ones attract each other. And this also explains why some relationships work, while others end up in divorce and betrayal. It's a long known principle in science.

Dr. Hideki Yukawa (Nobel Prize in Physics) discovered way back in 1935, that neutrons and protons in the nucleus of the atom (together called nucleons) constantly emit "virtual particles" called "mesons" and that they exchange these mesons with another nucleon (proton) or with themselves, and this interaction is what creates the "strong force" that holds the nucleus of the atom (and therefore all of physical reality) together.

In order to create this strong force, protons (nucleons) emit the virtual meson particles toward other like-particles in order to attract them into, or keep them in the nucleus of an atom.

The action and result created by this exchange of virtual particles among like-particles is that "strong force" itself — the strong force would not exist without this exchange of virtual particles. "The visible world is the invisible organization of energy" (Heinz Pagels - Physicist).

Those that don't have spiritual awareness, are like empty jars of invisible forms, manifesting what their impulses lead them to, out of any self-control or discipline.

We live in a world of consciousness and deprivation of self-consciousness, a world of living matter, in which all frequencies interact to bring us our life experience, as well as our own understanding of life.

This evidence has already been recognized thousands of years ago, even though mankind forgets the ultimate truth that all matter comes from a primary substance, a creative force, calling into existence all forms of life, in unending cycles of life and death. "All visible things arise from that which is invisible" (Bhagavad Gita, 6:2).

"So astounding are the facts in this connection that it would seem as though the Creator, himself, had electrically designed this planet just for the purpose of enabling us to achieve wonders" (Nikola Tesla).

Following this understanding, we know today that, with the right spiritual attitude, it is possible to open cosmic gates to higher dimensions, and evolve into higher frequency domains above the 3rd dimension, namely, a 4th, 5th, 6th and beyond.

"There is a collective entanglement of the frequencies of all life's energy. It is this string that ties the past to the future, one unconsciousness to another's' consciousness from one dimension to all the others, from here to the infinite, from a thought to a reality, from a vibration to a manifestation, from the beginning to the never ending (Simon Crowne).

"The distinction between past, present and future, is only a stubbornly persistent illusion" (Albert Einstein).

"The joy of life consists in the exercise of one's energies, continual growth, constant change, the enjoyment of every new experience. To stop means to simply die" (Aleister Crowley).

Chapter 60: How the Subconscious Determines Your Fate.

As Earth itself resonates into a higher frequency, we do move into a new and more uplifting level of existence and manifestations.

We attract everything that we manifest, and the acknowledgment of the principles within this Law of Attraction, depends on how we perceive such truth within a subdivision of multiple perspectives.

The lessons we face with a reincarnation in different worlds, each with a unique space-time continuum, assist in the need to recognize that "the imperishable is the invisible substance of all that is visible" (Bhagavad Gita, 6:23).

In this sense, it is interesting how we often attract people that match both what we need and reject the most. For those who study the Law of Attraction know that, in order to attract a soul-mate, a person must resonate emotions that correspond clearly to the image and characteristics of such soul.

"Choice, is what presents us with a multitude of paths, because choice creates a flow of electrons through the brain in a manner that inexorably leads to quantum superposition, and the many-worlds that are the inevitable result.

Our subconscious mind is aware of the 'many-worlds' coexisting simultaneously, and chooses a reality for us to continue to exist based on our self-concept" (Kevin Michel).

Either we are conscious of our decisions or not, we tend to attract people that resonate in the same frequency as us, while those that dream about finding a person of a different frequency, that will eventually change them and their life, tend to end up alone or with someone giving them the feeling of a non-existent perfection in relationships.

Relationships, as our body, are perfect in themselves, unless we promote imperfection with our unhealthy habits.

The common belief in what regards love, as being unreachable, doesn't correspond to love but to the frequency emitted instead. For in order to attract the one we want, we must first resonate in the same frequency of that desired ideal.

Conscious desire will lead us to daydreaming, which will then guide us into illusion, where we find ourselves believing the unreal in order to create that which will be real.

The difference between a dream and what we consider real, is actually the same between potential reality and optional reality.

Within the spectrum of our spiritual nature, it is impossible to dream about something we can't have or didn't have before.

"Science and psychology have isolated the one prime cause for success or failure in life. It is the hidden self-image you have of yourself" (Bob Proctor). For how could a dog attract another dog if expressing the nature of a cat or a bird?

We always attract what we need and not what we want, if wanting comes from the purpose of needing.

We also tend to want what we reject, and therefore, we typically reject our wishes.

How can a selfish person attract love, if his frequency isn't resonating towards acceptance and giving?

This person will attract a selfish person and then say to him or her:

— "You are selfish", Even though this individual was attracted by selfish desires.

The fact is that, the purpose of wanting someone, is in itself a selfish desire.

A person that loves doesn't want anything, but merely to give.

We can therefore resume the art of loving as the art of giving without need.

It doesn't matter what we do or who we are, because if we can't give in an altruistic manner, we can't truly love. Love is the perception of giving without possessing.

Before we desire to have someone to love, we must first love ourselves and emanate a similar energy, so that we may then find a person that truly loves us.

It is impossible to emanate a frequency related to lack of self-love and then attract a person with a different frequency, giving us what we don't give ourselves.

Chapter 61: How to Assimilate Your Emotions.

Emotions have a frequency and frequency has sound.

You know which frequency you are tapping into, when sound stimulates certain feelings and special mental reactions, namely, memories.

Tests have been conducted focusing on the effect of sound in patients, in what is known as the Six Solfeggio Frequencies, and the results include the following:

- UT 396 Hz — Liberating Guilt and Fear;
- RE 417 Hz — Undoing Situations and Facilitating Change;
- MI 528 Hz — Transformation and Miracles (DNA Repair);
- FA 639 Hz — Connecting/Relationships;
- SOL 741 Hz — Awakening/Intuition;
- LA 852 Hz — Returning to the Spiritual Order.

We should ask ourselves which frequency we are often connecting with:

- Sadness, depression, apathy and anger?
- Or, happiness, creativity and enlightenment?

As an example, music that can make you dream, imagine, work, and, in general, feel energetic and active, raises your frequency into a more uplifting level. But sounds that calm your mind, can help in reconnecting to your spirit.

"Focused low-frequency sound cancels the force of gravity, known to the ancients as the syllable 'Om'" (De Aquino, 2000).

Many followers of Buddhism have reported their benefits when meditating under visualization, and many Buddhists in Asia have been using the same process to help their followers, when praying for them.

As the Rig Veda says, "Meditate on the beautiful light of God, and may it stimulate our thoughts" (3:62).

The best way to meditate should then include relaxing sounds and visualizations that, when combined, can lead us into the answers we need from life.

"The whole universe is sustained by the divine syllable, Aum, which flows everywhere" (The Vedas 1:8), showing that God can manifest within our mind to guide our life.

This vibration is more naturally manifested by nature, and it is by connecting to it, that we connect to God's conscience effectively. The "God of Nature... adores all who adore Him" (The Vedas 1:10).

"All matter originates and exists only by virtue of a force which brings the particle of an atom to vibration and holds this most minute solar system of the atom together. We must assume behind this force the existence of a conscious and intelligent mind. This mind is the matrix of all matter" (Max Planck).

"Even matter called inorganic, believed to be dead, responds to irritants and gives unmistakable evidence of a living principle within.

Everything that exists, organic or inorganic, animated or inert, is susceptible to stimulus from the outside... Of all the frictional resistance, the one that most retards human movement is ignorance, what Buddha called "the greatest evil in the world".

The friction which results from ignorance can be reduced only by the spread of knowledge and the unification of the heterogeneous elements of humanity. No effort could be better spent...

Science is but a perversion of itself unless it has as its ultimate goal the betterment of humanity" (Nikola Tesla). For "as far as the laws of mathematics refer to reality, they are not certain, and as far as they are certain, they do not refer to reality" (Albert Einstein).

Chapter 62: Earthing Therapy.

Modern lifestyle has increasingly separated humans from the primordial flow of Earth's electrons. Rossi (1989) says that the use of insulating materials in post-World War II shoes has separated us from the Earth's energy field.

"Since the late 20th century, chronic degenerative diseases have overcome infectious disease as the major causes of death in the 21st century" (De Flora et al., 2005).

"Blood should flow like red wine — smoothly and easily, too many people have thicker blood, more like ketchup. That takes a lot more effort from the heart to circulate, and the pressure against the inside of arteries and blood vessels is much higher" (Dr. Sinatra, Founder of Heart MD Institute).

Researches have shown that a body suffering from pain has a deficiency of electrons, and this causes the blood cells to attach to one another in an effort to get the electrical charge that they need. And, unfortunately, this clumping act brings about an inflammatory, free-radical response – which causes pain.

According to Dr. Sinatra, you should "allow the Earth's free electrons to enter the body, where they synchronize all of your bioelectrical systems and powerfully reduce inflammation.

The sicker you are, the more you need to ground. Indications are that Earthing is indeed a natural solution to thinning the blood".

Ober (2000), a retired cable television executive, found a similarity between the human body (a bioelectrical, signal-transmitting organism) and the cable used to transmit cable television signals. When cables are "grounded" to the Earth, interference is virtually eliminated from the signal.

All electrical systems are stabilized by grounding them to the Earth.

Grounding the human body represents a "universal regulating factor in Nature" that strongly influences bioelectrical, bioenergetic and biochemical processes, and appears to offer a significant modulating effect on chronic illnesses (K. Sokal and P. Sokal, 2011).

We know today that the simple act of bare footing on Earth's soil or putting the palms of our hands in a tree rooted to Earth, decreases the impact of radiation in the body to nearly 100%, even if we are, at the same time, in contact with radioactive materials, such as the smartphone or a computer, not to mention the benefits we receive in our state of mind.

Most experts say that just 15 minutes of direct contact with Earth is all it takes to see profound benefits.

Earthing the human body is as essential to health as sunshine, clean air and water, nutritious food and physical activity.

"Since the beginning of creation there has been a flow of energy between our bodies and Mother Earth that works to support the various systems in our body and scavenge up free radicals that promote inflammation. More specifically, there is a flow of electrons through direct skin contact with the earth's surface.

Our planet has a negative electrical potential that is generated by solar winds, our ionosphere and lightning storms. When our skin is in direct contact with the Earth, we maintain the same electrical potential as our planet.

This phenomenon has been occurring mostly without interference up until the last several generations" (Kelly Pepper D.C., In Naturalnews).

Other habits related to increasing contact with Earth's frequency include "eating it".

Ancient civilizations, from all corners of the planet, knew that the simple habit of drinking clay could help completely detox the body.

The first recorded use of medicinal clay goes back to ancient Egypt and Mesopotamia (2500 BC) as anti-inflammatory agent and antiseptic.

The Ebers Papyrus (1500 BC) describes its application for a wide variety of purposes, including for intestinal problems and various eye complaints.

"Clays can eliminate excess grease and toxins from skin, and hence are very effective against dermatological diseases such as boils, acne, ulcers, abscess, and seborrhea" (Carretaro et al., 2006).

Recent studies show that the same process can also help eliminate radioactive particles inside the body. "In the stomach, the negative electrical charges of tiny clay particles attract positively charged toxins from stomach fluids. This clumping prevents very small particles, such as toxic molecules, from passing through the walls of the intestines and entering the bloodstream." (Suzanne Ubick, In The Magazine of the California Academy of Sciences, 2005).

Considering that all elements of life emit a certain frequency, we can conclude that all that is Earth-related, or somehow connected to its frequency, promotes life by reinforcing our DNA and protecting it.

Studies on Earthing Therapy, for example, have shown benefits for,...

- Allergies; Asthma; Arthritis; Autism;

- Chronic sinusitis; Cancer; Depression; Dementia;

- Heart disease;

- Obesity;

- Osteoporosis;

- Auto-immune diseases, such as Lupus, Rheumatoid Arthritis, Multiple Sclerosis, fibromyalgia and Type 1 diabetes.

Moreover, the Earth's frequency also protects against electromagnetic fields (EMFs), power lines, home wiring, airport and military radar, substations and transformers, while increasing our energy and vitality, reducing inflammation and oxidation, boosting intelligence, regulating blood pressure, alleviating skin conditions and improving longevity.

Until recent times, people lived in a close daily contact with the Earth. They walked barefoot on the ground and slept close to or directly on the Earth.

Ancient healers believed Earth's energy could be easily absorbed through our skin and through the soles of our feet.

It wouldn't make sense to talk about a Spiritual DNA without fist understanding its effects on our Biological DNA, as spirit and body interact as one. "The cosmos is within us. We are made of star-stuff. We are a way for the universe to know itself" (Carl Sagan).

Practicing ground therapy, can then rebalance the electrical charges pulsing through our body, which improves intercellular communication, reduces deadly inflammation, helps all our systems to function better and leads to more optimal health.

Chapter 63: Why We Are What We Eat.

The more we consume foods closer to Earth's frequencies, the healthier we become.

"Modern anthropological data support this: all cultures and peoples show a preference for animal foods and animal fat" (Stephen Byrnes - nutritionist and naturopathic doctor).

However, "their foods did not contain preservatives, additives, or colorings. They did not contain added sugar, white flour or canned foods.

Their milk products were not pasteurized, homogenized, or low fat. The animal and plant foods consumed were raised and grown on pesticide-free soil and were not given growth hormones or antibiotics.

In short, these people always ate organic" (Stephen Byrnes).

It is difficult to see someone reaching 100 years old in a modern civilization, where food is mainly genetically modified or processed, and people consume products from brands receiving investments from major Pharmaceutical and Health Insurance Companies.

"U.S. and Canadian health insurance giants own nearly $2 billion worth of stock in fast food giants like McDonald's, Burger King, KFC, Taco Bell and others" (Mike Adams), while "Pharmaceutical Companies are running a $280 billion money making scam" (Michael Snyder).

"Drug fatalities more than doubled among teens and young adults between 2000 and 2008. Deaths more than tripled among people aged 50 to 69.

In terms of sheer numbers, the death is highest among people in their 40s" (Los Angeles Times).

A more specific example, is the Swiss Multinational food and beverage company Nestlé, which owns Insurance, Pharmaceutical and Cosmetic Companies.

We are being constantly exposed to chemicals, while disdaining their secondary effects, such as stroke, cancer and many other diseases, often originating in a deregulation of our DNA molecule.

"Today, more than 95% of all chronic disease is caused by food choice, toxic food ingredients, nutritional deficiencies and lack of physical exercise" (Mike Adams).

"Foods of modern commerce do not provide sufficient nutrients to allow the body to reach its full genetic potential — neither the complete development of the bones in the body and the head, nor the fullest expressions of the various systems that allow humankind to function at optimal levels — immune system, nervous system, digestion, and reproduction" (Sally Fallon).

"Hawaiians who ate their traditional diet of coconut, fish, shellfish, taro, sweet potatoes, and fresh fruits were healthy and strong. Today, however, the health of native Hawaiians is frightening. Obesity and diabetes are rampant" (Stephen Byrnes, Nutritionist and Naturopathic Doctor).

It is estimated that 70% of all physical diseases are psychosomatic, which means our diet can be attributed to merely 30% of them, often labeled as chronic.

In essence, we could say that the body heals and rebuilds itself, if exposed to the right ingredients and environmental conditions.

"Natural forces within us are the true healers of disease" (Hippocrates).

It is normal to assume that a real doctor should "cure and prevent disease with nutrition" (Thomas Edison).

Many studies have shown how cancer, diabetes and high blood pressure, can be healed with a diet consisting only of a wide variety of raw vegetables. Just like Hippocrates said: "Let food be thy medicine and medicine be thy food."

As an example, we can consider Vitamin B1, or Thiamine, which has been used in many anti-radiation therapies to clean the body of its toxins. Thiamine can be found in beans, rice, vegetables, orange and lemon.

Another example, to illustrate this, is related to the Hawaii Diet, composed of "fish, taro, sweet potatoes, fresh fruit and vegetables, and, occasionally, pork. Specifically avoided are white rice, sugar, Spam, and processed foods in general.

The change is dramatic: people lose weight, they have more energy, and their health problems dissipate or become more manageable. Their teeth invariably improve as well" (Stephen Byrnes).

Similarities can be found in Asian cultures, where about 90% to 100% of the diet is based on vegetables, from both land and sea. Diets rich in seaweed, for example, are rich in iodine, needed for the normal metabolism of cells and converting food into energy.

Dr. David Brownstein found that 100% of all his tested patients with cancer where deficient in this mineral, which can be found also in cod fish, sea salt or iodized salt, shrimp, tuna and egg.

This mineral is common among Japanese. "60 million mainland Japanese consume a daily average of 13.8 mg of elemental iodine in the form of seaweed, and they are one of the healthiest nations based on overall well-being and cancer statistics.

A deficiency of iodine, increases risk for thyroid cancer, breast cancer, ovarian cancer, uterine cancer, endometrial cancer, and prostate cancer.

The Japanese consume 100 times the recommended RDA. They have the lowest incidence of breast cancer in the world" (In joannebrophy.com).

"Virtually no one in the field of health and nutrition speaks about the concept of food having energy, but if you stop and think about it, it intuitively makes sense. Vegetables have a lighter energy than proteins.

Animal meat from tortured animals has a different energy than meat from animals that lived a peaceful existence" (Joshua Rosenthal, Founder and Director of the Institute for Integrative Nutrition).

Chapter 64: How Frequencies Heal The Body.

Nearly 100 years ago, Nicola Tesla focused certain frequencies on afflicted areas of Patients and in some cases sited them in the vicinity of vibrations from a device called Lakhovsky Multiwave Oscillator, which produced a blend of specific frequencies, and it is said they have experienced relief from rheumatism and other painful conditions.

This therapy was also considered a cure for certain types of paralysis. The radiation increased the supply of blood to the area with a warming effect (diathermy), enhancing the oxygenation and nutritive value of the blood, what led to an increase of various secretions and an acceleration in the elimination of waste products in the blood.

Electrotherapists, following Nicola Tesla principles, even spoke of broadcasting vitamins to the body and documented reversals of cancer tumor growths. But just like anything else in science, the future of these findings depends on who is using them and for which purpose.

Nicola Tesla is the father of wireless communication, pioneering Internet, Radio, Mobile Phones and Remote Control Devices. And even though his intentions may have been good, they have allowed the creation of the Radio-Frequency Identification.

RFID microchips started being implanted in humans by Conrad Chase Night Clubs, in Spain and Holland, to identify VIP customers, in 2004.

Later on, Hospitals own by Centrak Enterprise, started using them to collect data from badges worn by patients and employees.

The same idea was adopted by Singapore.

Nowadays, a large number of U.S. Hospitals implant patients with RFID microchips, to incorporate personal medical information. And the next step of this "revolutionary" technology will be neurologic implants, or brain implants, that will cure chronic diseases and enable the disabled to live normal lives.

This revolution will allow losing weight in a matter of days, or download an entire college course into the memory within hours.

The possibilities are endless and it's just a matter of time before having a Brain Implanted Microchip becomes as fashionable as the new iPhones.

According to The Financial Times, the Pharmaceutical Company of the future will include a "bioelectronics" business that "treats disease through electrical signaling in the brain and elsewhere", allowing diseases such as diabetes and epilepsy, and conditions such as obesity and depression, to be treated "through electronic implants into the brain rather than pills or injections".

Moncef Slaoui — head of research and development at the British pharmaceutical giant GlaxoSmithKline — says that the "challenge is to integrate the work – in brain- computer interfaces, materials science, nanotechnology, micro-power generation – to provide therapeutic benefit".

In 2012, Mashable released an article mentioning that "rats showed motor function in formerly damaged gray matter after a neural microchip was implanted under the rat's skull and electrodes were transferred to the rat's brain. Without the microchip, rats with damaged brain tissue did not have motor function.

Both strokes and Parkinson's can cause permanent neurological damage to brain tissue, so this scientific research brings hope".

In other words, "Imagine there's a small area in the brain that is malfunctioning and imagine that we understand the architecture of this damaged area. So we try to replicate this part of the brain with electronics" (Matti Mintz, Professor at Tel Aviv University).

Pharmaceutical companies haven't increase life expectancy, or at least not while maintaining diseases from which people suffer all their lives with. So why should they have direct power over our brain and our lives in the future?

A person that can make us happy and productive with the push of a button, can also kill us faster with the same technology, giving meaning to the biblical quote that says that "as many as would not worship the image of the beast should be killed" (Revelation 13:15).

Chapter 65: The Plan to Enslave of Humankind.

What kind of life will we have, when the natural vibration of our soul is completely disrupted by signals blocking the manifestation of our spirituality?

The answer can be found in an article from the Wall Street Journal (2012), mentioning that "a neural implant can essentially "listen" to your brain activity and then "talk" directly to your brain".

According to Computer World UK (2009), "eventually people may be willing to be more committed to brain implants", as "by the year 2020, you won't need a keyboard and mouse to control your computer. Instead, users will open documents and surf the web using nothing more than their brain waves".

This certainly represents astonishing news for all those that have always mocked and disregarded the possibility of telepathy between human beings, or even between them and animals, as Intel Research Scientist Dean Pomcrlcau supports his investigation based on the fact that "if two people think of the image of a bear or hear the word bear or even hear a bear growl, a neuroimage would show similar brain activity.

Basically, there are standard patterns that show up in the brain for different words or images. You could compose characters or words by thinking about letters flashing on the screen or typing whole words rather than their individual characters".

This technology can also be used "to operate computers, television sets and cell phones. The brain waves would be harnessed with Intel-developed sensors implanted in people's brains" (Computer World UK, 2009). "If you just need to think about calling someone, it happens. Or you can control the cursor on a computer screen just by thinking about where you want to move it.

Scientists in the field of bioinformatics have designed headsets with advanced sensors to read electrical brain activity that can recognize facial expressions, excitement and concentration levels, and thoughts of a person without them physically taking any actions.

We will begin to see early applications of this technology in the gaming and entertainment industry. IBM is developing technology that uses real-time analytics to make sense and integrate data from across all the facets of your life such as your social networks and online preferences to present and recommend information that is only useful to you" (IBM.com, 2011).

"The first human-to-human, brain-to-brain noninvasive interface has been created by researchers at the University of Washington. The system allows one researcher to remotely control the hand of another researcher across the internet, merely by thinking about moving his hand.

The researchers are already looking at a two-way system, to allow for a more "equitable" telepathic link between the two human brains, and the telepathic communication of complex information" (in extremetech.com, 2013).

Merely a month before Intel's research is made public, Professor Charlets Higgins, from the University of Arizona, reported that he had successfully built a robot that is guided by the brain and eyes of a moth and predicted that in 10 to 15 years people will be using "hybrid" computers running a combination of technology and living organic tissue.

Chapter 66: What Future Can We Expect?

There are currently approximately 100,000 people worldwide with implants in their brains, most of those for medical reasons, but the U.S. Government intends to "spend more than $70 million over five years to jump to the next level of brain implants" (The Boston Globe Journal).

The implications to our understanding of reality and the world will significantly impact the way we perceive our life.

As Google CEO Larry Page said in an interview to Steven Levy, "When you think about something and don't really know much about it, you will automatically get information. Eventually you'll have an implant, where if you think about a fact, it will just tell you the answer".

As researchers expect that consumers will want the freedom they will gain by using the implant, according to Michael Snyder, "at some point in the future, having a brain implant may be as common as it is to use a smartphone today" (Infowars.com).

For those that have always doubted the principles behind the Law of attraction, mocked or doubt it, this new technology will certainly prove it real.

It is relevant to notice that Intel "has used Functional Magnetic Resonance Imaging (FMRI) machines to determine that blood flow changes in specific areas of the brain based on what word or image someone is thinking of, showing that people tend to show the same brain patterns for similar thoughts" (Computer World UK, 2009).

However, "implantable microchips that can "talk" directly to the brain would give a tyrannical government the ultimate form of control. If you could download thoughts and feelings directly into the brains of your citizens, you could achieve total control and never have to worry that they would turn on you.

You could potentially program these chips to make your citizens feel good all the time. You could have these chips produce a "natural high" that never ends.

That would make your citizens incredibly dependent on the chips and they would never want to give them up.

This kind of technology has the potential to be one of the greatest threats to liberty and freedom in the history of mankind.

At first these implantable microchips will be sold to us as one of the greatest "breakthroughs" ever, but in the end they could end up totally enslaving us" (Michael Snyder).

Life without the frequency of life isn't alive anymore, and that's the true nature of evil.

"Every conscious thought you have, every moment you spend on an idea, is a commitment to be stuck with that idea and with aspects of that level of thinking, for the rest of your life.

Spending just 10 seconds focusing on a topic that does not serve your interests is to invest your energy along a path that will continue to draw from you and define you" (Kevin Michel).

Companies like IBM, may be telling us otherwise, when referring that we "will be able to walk up to an ATM machine to securely withdraw money" (IBM.com, 2011), or check the account balance in our mobile phone or table with the same procedure, but the Bible has shown already a different perspective of this reality, when mentioning that in the future "no one can buy or sell unless he has the mark... on the right hand or the forehead ...and have no rest day nor night" (Revelation 13:16 / 14:11).

Chapter 67: TransHumanism.

Around 1900, at the turn of the twentieth century, Nikola Tesla was designing a "World System," anticipating a method of broadcasting music, speech, pictures, newspapers, and ship navigation signals to all parts of the globe.

Our society would become interconnected, thus advancing humanity's need to become more unified and live together in more peaceful and progressive ways.

In addition, he claimed that it would provide personal telephone communications between parties, regardless of distance, with an incredible device, small enough to be carried in one's pocket — a full century before anybody had ever heard of the Internet or cellular phones.

Nikola Tesla is the father of almost everything of what is today a reality, even though in his time was seen as a lunatic, whose experiments were worth only of being introduced in sci-fi movies.

The knowledge about how frequencies interact to process information, sound, images and movies, not only led to the creation of devices once seen as impossible to exist, such as the television, but also went as far as to what today is known as the iPhone and Wi-Fi.

It is definitely amazing how, with merely a certain frequency, we can get images, movies, music, text, and many more things, into our laptop computers.

Current researches in the field of nanotechnology show that the same principle can be applied to our brain, explaining how a neuro-implant can enhance our human capabilities and make our brain interact with computers.

Humans will become able to interact with the physical world by simply using their thoughts.

While resembling as much as possible our thought patterns and personal needs, in order to support our daily tasks, or even pleasurable moments, computers are becoming more like an indispensable machine in people's existence, as they aren't only tools for work anymore, but also communication and emotions.

Soon, computers and humans will become one single organism, in what is called the Era of TransHumanism.

"The Global Future 2045 International Congress, held in Moscow in 2012, lays out a stark vision of the future for neo-humanity where AI, cybernetics, nanotech and other emerging technologies replace mankind.

The group admittedly met to draft a "resolution that will be submitted to the United Nations, demanding the implementation of committees to discuss life extension Avatar projects as a necessary tool in the preservation of humankind."

- By 2025, the group foresees the creation of an autonomous system, providing life support for the brain, that is capable of 'interacting with the environment'; brains transplanted into avatar bodies greatly expanding life and allowing complete sensory experiences;

- 2040-2050 brings the arrival of bodies 'made of nano-robots' that can take any shape, as well as hologram bodies;

- 2045-2050 will bring forth drastic changes to the social structure and sci-tech development. It is in this age that the United Nation's original promise of the end to war and violence is again predicted" (in Infowars.com, 2012).

In this digital era, humans have become more adjusted to the procedure of using a computer and a smart phone for 24 hours a day, facilitating the possibility of telepathic communication between humans and machines.

Within this reality, technology can be seen as the method used to take control over our own frequency, life and thoughts.

Chapter 68: The World We Could Have.

Just like any other electronic device, our mind receives information related to the frequency we tune into. We don't need to have answers more than we need to wish them.

"Instinct is something which transcends knowledge. We have, undoubtedly, certain finer fibers that enable us to perceive truths when logical deduction, or any other willful effort of the brain, is futile" (Nikola Tesla).

However, it is naive to expect that wearing RFID Implants in our brains or hands will lead to more freedom, as history has shown a very different outcome for all the inventions that could have dramatically change the planet towards a more uplifting reality.

The Law of Attraction won't have the same meaning anymore, if we stop having ideas and dreaming.

The fundamental principle can be found inside the words of Nikola Tesla when he says: "When wireless is fully applied, the Earth will be converted into a huge brain, capable of response in every one of its parts".

If we substitute the words wireless by frequency, brain by energy field and parts by reality, we have the answer to the mechanics behind the Law of Attraction:

"When a frequency is fully applied, a human will be converted into a huge energy field, capable of response in any reality".

This frequency is the manifestation of our soul, our spiritual DNA, which gains its maximum potential when plugged to the energy field of God, found in Nature, and mainly in grounding habits and organic diets.

We can even rephrase the sentence by saying the following: "When spirituality if fully applied, the Earth will be converted into a huge energy field, capable of response in everyone and everything".

A pure soul can change the world. When we are living within the right frequency, our spiritual DNA, and the frequency of what we wish to obtain, while connected to Earth's energy field, we receive inspiring thoughts and ideas, leading us to create and work according to our mission on Earth.

This truth was mentioned by Tesla when he said: "The idea came like a flash of lightning and in an instant the truth was revealed... Ideas came in an uninterrupted stream and the only difficulty I had was to hold them fast."

Inspired humans bring to our world a new hope for a bright future. It is the evil mind of some, supported by the fear of others, that allows the distortion of those deeds into evil actions, while suppressing the manifestation of a beautiful reality.

The light of God inspires, while the darkness of the Devil suppresses.

Either a person believes or not in those entities, there's no doubt that only two forces are operating in this tridimensional world. And our spiritual DNA can only serve one of them. "No one can serve two masters. Either you will hate the one and love the other, or you will be devoted to the one and despise the other" (Matthew 6:24).

Chapter 69: How to Develop Self-Control.

Having needs, means resonating in a different frequency of that of having what we need. Therefore, you must find replacements to your needs, so that you may get the object of your desires, when not needing it anymore.

Source and energy nullify cause and effect, when what is, just is, in expansion with itself.

This is the principle behind meditation and the reason why it can be such a powerful exercise for the mind. "Your mind quiets down and your body is relaxed. You're still conscious, but you are able to get in touch with your subconscious" (Jose Silva). "Power would be transmitted by creating 'standing waves" (Nikola Tesla, 1932).

Almost 60 years before science could confirm its results, Nikola Tesla created an Earthquake in a city by accurately determining the resonant frequencies of the Earth and getting a steam-driven oscillator to vibrate at the same frequency as the ground.

This shows how powerful one can be, by simply going within a frequency that both promotes the expansion of our energy field and at the same time stops any external influence from entering our mind.

We can control nature as much we can control ourselves by the same laws, as we are all one.

This is what Buddha defined as the state of being without being, where all human needs can cease existing.

There isn't any wish or dream that can be seen as unreal or illogical, for we are spiritual beings with access to an infinite life-force, able to use such field of energy as a way to achieve life purpose.

"The gift of mental power comes from God, Divine Being, and if we concentrate our minds on that truth, we become in tune with this great power" (Nikola Tesla).

Discovering our life purpose is then as important as the fulfilling of our karmic experience, or the manifestation of our deepest desires.

Basically, before attracting the Ferrari of your dreams, you will attract first the experience that will allow gaining awareness of the reasons behind such need, and you will get it if you remain connected to such experience.

However, what you dream can also destroy you, if you can't understand why you have it after possessing it.

Dreams are related to our spiritual purpose and they lead us to a higher consciousness, in which material purposes are merely tools.

Nothing exists in the material world that wasn't first thought, and that's why "your greatest ability is getting an idea" (Ron Hubbard, Scientology).

If we confuse material illusions with spiritual purpose, then we'll be lost in the fire of desire, which increases through the emotions of greed and selfishness.

"A wise man, recognizing that the world is but an illusion, does not act as if it is real, so he escapes the suffering" (Buddha).

Following happiness is the same as following truth, and it is this truth that will reconnect us with the frequency of salvation, by leading us to the true meaning of our existence. If we can't recognize this truth, then we are already dead.

A person that can't accept his weaknesses to embrace truth, is afraid of destiny, but within that fear, sells his soul to those controlling it.

"Courage could be summed up in one, being willing to cause something and two, going ahead to achieve the effect one has postulated against any and all odds" (Ron Hubbard, Scientology).

Chapter 70: Should You Be Superstitious?

It is the believe in having what we dream without any doubts, that creates such reality.

Those who are successful in any field, didn't doubt that they would make it. And those who fail, doubt more than they can see solutions, and will always doubt more than the number of solutions they find.

The frequency that you apply, either for belief or doubt, is the same, meaning that the doubts can diminish the power of your beliefs.

As an example, when you show a solution to someone's problem, you tend to notice how many barriers that person puts in front of the solution, how many "maybes" and "not sures" he or she mentions.

If you keep showing solutions, you will proceed to see an increasing number of barriers, then in the form of excuses of any type. At the end, they will start to invalidate your beliefs and make you doubt yourself and your assumptions.

Why people do this? Because they are mentally blocked by their own beliefs.

Quite often, they don't think they have the money, the appearance, the time, or whatsoever it is, to accomplish what they want.

As people tend to make calculations for the future based on their memories of the past, they end up spending an entire life with their head inside a box. They can't see beyond that box.

They filter every opportunity coming their way because they cannot see it. They cannot see beyond their limiting beliefs. And so, they sabotage absolutely everything that happens and is positive. And end up going back to the same cycles they know.

Most people are not willing to do anything to get what they want. They may say they want something, but as I have seen, hundreds of times, in many countries, they never want to put the work where their mouth is. And "part of paying the price is the willingness to do whatever it takes to get the job done. It comes from a declaration that you are going to get it done no matter what it takes, no matter how long it takes, no matter what comes up" (Jack Canfield)

If you question them about what they want, you may even increase their potential to never getting it, especially, if they are already unwilling to make the necessary efforts to achieve it.

That is why many believe that, when sharing their wishes with friends, they attract bad luck. This bad luck is the equivalent to the amount of power in the frequency resonating from others.

Such superstition does make sense, but only to the extent that one lacks self-trust. For the opinion of others on you and your future, only applies to you if you can't control your mind.

If you are very weak, yes, anyone can influence you. But they are already doing it anyway, with their opinions and expectations.

It is simply not possible to escape the influence of the frequency of other people. You have to choose your friends and acquaintances well, if you want to make sure others don't have a negative impact on you.

Preferably, you will want to be the average of the people you hang out with, because you will be anyway.

Chapter 71: Can Your Friends Determine Your Future?

It is true that the less people wish to see you obtain what you want, the less likely you are to get it. This happens, because they are either jealous or afraid to lose you, or simply, because they don't believe you can achieve it.

Your friends and relatives tend to represent the strongest forces opposing your dreams, even if they are unconscious about it.

"Success depends on getting good at saying no without feeling guilty. You cannot get ahead with your own goals if you are always saying yes to someone else's projects. You can only get ahead with your desired lifestyle if you are focused on the things that will produce that lifestyle" (Jack Canfield).

When you share your dreams with people that don't believe in you, you are increasing the need for resonating at a stronger frequency, in the same proportion of the rejecting frequency they emanate. And "to get over rejection, you have to realize that rejection is really a myth. It doesn't really exist. It is simply a concept that you hold in your head.

Think about it! If you ask Patty to have dinner with you and she says no, you didn't have anyone to eat dinner with before you asked her, and you don't have anyone to eat dinner with after you asked her" (Jack Canfield).

The three main reasons for people to emanate a negative frequency opposing your goals, are,...

- Believing that they'll be less meaningful in your life;

- Believing that you'll disappear from their life forever;

- Believing that you don't deserve what you want and shouldn't get it.

In other words, it is not only about your self-image that you should be worried about, but also the image others have of you, as both affect your life in a very determinant way, reason why people have so many difficulties to change.

Commonly, the only way to make a significant change in your life, implies the risk of losing everything you have, including your friends and the support of your family. And so, "never regret yesterday. Life is in you today, and you make your tomorrow" (Ron Hubbard, Scientology).

Those who take the highest risks and change the most tend to end up alone. But, "When you're 18, you worry about what everybody is thinking of you; when you're 40, you don't give a darn what anybody thinks of you; when you're 60, you realize nobody's been thinking about you at all" (Dr. Daniel Amen).

People only think about themselves, and what they wish or don't for your life, is related to their expectations.

Unless you're living your own life, with the risk of tremendous loss and conflicts, you are surely living somebody else's life.

Most individuals are nothing more than the result of the beliefs of those within their closest social circle. For nobody wants to have a friend that either shows weaknesses and failures, or unveils our own worse attributes.

That is why people are so similar. They reflect each other because they want to belong and fit in. They don't want to be seen as failures.

Chapter 72: Success is a Lonely Road.

Your reality is the resulting combination of the frequencies — either positive or negative — of those who know you, when combined with your own self-image.

Every thought resonates in a certain frequency that is interconnected with the thoughts of everyone else.

This means that we get what we want in the direct proportion of what we don't need, the unawareness of others and the strength of our beliefs.

Every single thing in our reality fits within this equation. Therefore, it is easier to get what nobody expects from you. But also, if you are very determined in your goals, you will certainly lose friends.

This is obvious, due to the idea everyone you know has of you, and which quite often is far inferior that what you would expect. "Basically, your potentialities are a great deal better than anyone ever permitted you to believe" (Ron Hubbard, Scientology).

One of the biggest mistakes a person can make, consists in expecting the approval of others to fulfill dreams, or even expecting their recognition. Because they neglect the fact that it may never happen.

I have experience with success in many areas, from music to writing, and I travel a lot. And despite my background and awards, I still see the same patterns wherever I go:

- Nobody believes anything that is outside their comfort zone, even if they never saw it, and someone else has it;

- People always judge you according to what they think your value is, and not your real value, meaning that they ignore your achievements to focus on your appearance;

- Everyone has the brain of an insect, which means that they cannot project any thought into the future. As soon as you tell them when you are going to leave their city, they invalidate the friendship.

Alone you have more chances of getting what you want, for "an individual must rise above an avid craving for agreement from a humanoid group to get anything decent done" (Ron Hubbard, Scientology).

That is actually the greatest challenge in pursuing your dreams — your loneliness. But loneliness is not only about being alone. Loneliness is also about,...

- Working long hours alone;

- Working while being ridiculed by others for what you chose to do;

- Working while your spouse or girlfriend decides to betray you;

- Working despite your emotions, either it is sadness, stress, anxiety or fear;

But most importantly,...

- Celebrating alone.

In fact, if people ever praise you, is only at the end. Because they only want the result of what you accomplish.

If you depend on their emotional support, you will never go anywhere.

What makes winners succeed, is precisely the fact that they would do what they do, under any condition.

The vast majority of the people can only believe what they see, but they see what they want to see.

Television is their god, and through this machine they accept values, implanted to control their minds and the minds of others around them.

That is their world. And if we allow them to determine our thoughts and decisions, we get sucked in into that world of theirs.

The fear of losing social credibility, being mocked or ridiculed, is what keeps people within the same system. Bullying is part of it. And it doesn't happen only in schools.

Whenever you refuse to comfort to the norm, you will be bullied and harassed in some way.

- That is why stay home moms, are ridiculed by society;

- That is why people of a black skin who drive Lamborghinis are stopped by the police;

- That is why whenever I work with my laptop in public places, everyone looks at me as if I was committing a crime, especially, in countries where most habitants are dumb retards, I.e., Lithuania, Poland, Spain and Portugal.

Chapter 73: How to Become a Magnet to Success.

The frequency of self-esteem and self-determination is the strongest, reason why such individuals will always be rejected by society, fired from many jobs and even insulted and humiliated.

That is the destiny of the greatest throughout history.

They are the greatest because the most powerful frequency, emanating from a strong determinism, is found in action. It is the exact opposite of apathy, where most people find themselves in any moment in time.

In essence, you are either changing the world with your will, or dying inside of it. Because, in between, all you have are those who are forced into action to survive.

Most people hate their job and their life in general.

Our world is being simultaneously maintained, destroyed and promoted:

- Maintained by those who fear change;

- Destroyed by those who fear development and profit from the destruction;

- Promoted by those who, through positive action, want to change their life by improving their world.

Quite clearly, the vast majority of the population fears change. And those who profit from their unwillingness to change, profit the most, and find themselves fearing development.

Such is the case of,...

- The Pharmaceutical Companies;

- The Military Industry;

- The politicians.

The ones who remain, at the top of this social hierarchy, are few and rarely appreciated. They are the entrepreneurs, the artists, the writers, and the independent inventors and researchers.

In such a world, "there is only one way you will ever have a future: make one" (Ron Hubbard, Scientology).

How can we then attract wealth if the vast majority of the planet is going on the opposite direction?

To understand the answer to this question, you must change your idea of wealth, because it is their idea, and not the real one.

You see, I have done many things that people consider to be impossible, including making more money as a full-time author than I ever did before, with any job, or even the accumulation of jobs.

The vast majority of the people I encounter, in any country, still don't believe I am a full-time author, because their reality is incompatible to mine.

The way they look at money is the way of the masses. Which is also a no-way, as the masses know nothing about money.

In reality, attracting money is as realistic as attracting people or attracting a cup of coffee. It follows the exact same principles. "Money is the simplest thing in the world once you learn how to do it. It's like driving a car. It's simple if you know how to do it" (Bob Proctor).

Here is what I have learned about making money as an author, musician and entrepreneur, that matches any other activity:

- You always need a plan, either it is a job, going out with friends, or starting a business;

- You need to know how to analyze your results, to keep a job, know who is a real friend and who's not, and to make sure a business does not fail;

- You should not be afraid to restart, either it is about correcting your mistakes at work (or finding a new job), apologizing to others for your behaviors (or finding new friends), or restarting your business (or a new business).

These principles seem simple, but in my case, as an author, I can tell you that,…

- My plan included 10 years of a tremendous amount of working hours, and the acceptance of jobs that didn't pay me much, but allowed me to spend more time writing;

- Analyzing my results meant spending many hours studying the market and its possibilities, and travel between countries to solve issues related to different banks. I opened more than 20 bank accounts in three different continents, before I finally decided which ones to work with;

- Not being afraid to restart is now basically part of my life, as I change country every 6 months.

As you noticed by my examples, I created my future with determinism, planning and plenty of hard work. Because "future is the creation of a future illusion and the working toward that illusion to make it a reality" (Ron Hubbard, Scientology).

In the end, "the greatest discovery you'll ever make, is the potential of your own mind" (Jose Silva).

Chapter 74: Emotions and Money.

We attract what is in the same frequency we feel, and our emotions build that energy field. In scientific terms, "protons give an atom its identity, electrons its personality" (Bill Bryson).

Our relationship with money is affected by our own beliefs about money. This is why we tend to feel that, when we want or need something, we can't have it, but when we don't want or need it anymore, we get it.

We could also say that, the more we need something, the less we are in the same frequency of getting it. "If your only goal is to become rich, you will never achieve it" (John D. Rockefeller, World's first Billionaire).

No wonder most rich people avoid the poor, as if avoiding the plague. They fear being affected by need.

It is when you are completely within the emotion of having an object, that you don't need it anymore. That is the meaning of getting things when you least expect, or being lucky. And that is also why so many people say:

- "I always get what I want when I least expect";
- "I always get what I want when I don't need it anymore";
- "God only gives me when I am ready to receive it."

It is when you don't need something that you get it. But you can only stop needing it when your focus moves to the emotion of having it.

"All of the great achievers of the past have been visionary figures; they were men and women who projected into the future. They thought of what could be, rather than what already was, and then they moved themselves into action, to bring these things into fruition" (Bob Proctor).

The more you can experience the frequency within the reality of having what you want, which is perceived with emotions and thoughts, the stronger and faster is your power to attract it.

"The more we delve into quantum mechanics, the stranger the world becomes; appreciating this strangeness of the world, whilst still operating in that which you now consider reality, will be the foundation for shifting the current trajectory of your life from ordinary to extraordinary.

It is the Tao of mixing this cosmic weirdness with the practical and physical, which will allow you to move, moment by moment, through parallel worlds to achieve your dreams" (Kevin Michel).

In this journey towards our dreams, our biggest enemies are our negative emotions and limiting thoughts.

Those who can't achieve their dreams of wealth and abundance, tend to think "I don't deserve it", "I can't do it" or "I will fail", while feeling fear, anxiety, depression and sadness.

We may need to reprogram our thoughts with a self-loving belief, and our heart with self-loving emotions, before reaching anything in life. It consists of saying "I can do it and I deserve it" in front of a mirror, and until we believe in those words, while doing the things we love and that make us feel happy.

The only way to change our life is with inspired actions, and towards our ideal lifestyle, using persistence and consistency.

Nicola Tesla said that the primary substance, thrown into infinitesimal whirls of prodigious velocity, becomes gross matter, but if the motion ceases, then matter disappears, reverting to the primary substance.

In other words, the strongest energy a person can emanate comes from the thought of deserving what is wished, so that it becomes possible to believe in the right to have it.

"Thoughts become things. If you see it in your mind, you will hold it in your hand" (Bob Proctor).

Rich people believe that God gives them their wealth, and that they have the right to have it. "God gave me my money", said John D. Rockefeller.

In order to develop such deserving feelings, we must first build the spiritual base that supports them, such as clarifying the reasons as to why we deserve the amount of wealth we wish to receive from the Universe.

"The power to make money is a gift of God, to be developed and used to the best of our ability for the good of mankind" (John D. Rockefeller).

Chapter 75: The Potential to Become Wealthy.

The fundamental difference between those who have the potential for success and wealth, and those who don't, is in their frequency. Everyone has an energy that either attract or repels these things. And we can see it in their habits.

People of lower energy levels will always feel good inside crowded places, like shopping malls, parties and riots, and they are the majority.

The minority is driven by purpose when inside such environments, and not magnetic pulsations or emotions. And they will avoid them when feeling negative, because it doesn't match their nature, namely, when feeling weak, sick, angry or stupid.

These feelings don't just describe what we can feel in environments of a lower nature, but also what we can see in the attitudes and actions of individuals promoting such magnetic fields. Criticism, insults, ridicule, discrimination, obsession, manipulation, selfishness, arrogance, jealousy, guilt tripping, gossiping and aggression, are all common behaviors seen in negative individuals.

It must be known as well that negativity is correlated to fear and anxiety, which are the most common emotions in society.

It is then expectable that anyone, unaware of this knowledge or, while aware, failing in controlling his own emotions, may rapidly change his personality and turn into a completely different person, unrecognizable and distinct from the previous.

It is indeed as if we were living in a world of zombies and vampires, where each one of us becomes one of them, after being bitten and contaminated with the negative energy of those that already have such nature.

The strong attachment to material objects or physical recognition, like money and popularity, makes most people become extremely vulnerable to a negative transmutation within their soul.

"In the great majority of mankind there is such a preponderance of selfishness and a desire to get the most out of life as they view that matter, that either they are busy keeping the wolf from the door or accumulating possessions and taking care of them, and hence they have very little time or inclination to undertake the soul culture so necessary to true success in life" (Max Heindel, Rosicrucian Fellowship).

Our attitude towards life determines life's reflections towards us. If your brainwaves are in lower levels, it means that so is your body, leading you to become more vulnerable to diseases, anger and stress, which in turn make you vulnerable to lack of self-control.

It is not a coincidence that, when near negative individuals, we tend to get sick, angry and even violent.

Most psychologists are unaware that mental disorders are contagious and have affected their mind and work. And so, it is not a coincidence as well, that most therapists tend to lose the potential to efficiently analyze a problem in their patients over the years.

An individual affected by negative frequency waves, operates with a logic that doesn't necessarily solve a problem. It is a process that guides the mind without self-awareness or critical thinking, a skill that education intends to develop in citizens, while suppressing the ability to analyze situations from different perspectives and the innate skill of problem-solving with creativity.

The suppression of thought is such in the modern world, that we now commonly find many psychologists and psychiatrists under the effect of some type of drug, from medications for allergies, vaccines and vitamins to antidepressants. And these would be the best cases among them, as these are also some of the careers with the highest suicide rate.

Thought is affected by energy. We can't escape the magnetic field around us. The people that are closest to you, such as neighbors, colleagues and friends, as well as everyone else that you encounter when using public transportation, affect your energy field.

Those that know it, have always, throughout history, tried to be apart from society, in their castles and palaces positioned in isolated locations.

This magnetic field is constantly in interaction, and our brainwaves, as well as our thoughts, are reflections of it.

Chapter 76: The Social Implications of TransHumanism.

The introduction of the RFID microchip will bring to the Power Elite the possibility of controlling and monitoring thoughts and energy frequencies, as well as manipulate them, transforming humanity into a community of idealistic slaves as never before seen in our history.

Most people are completely unaware of the dangers of having smartphones, or RFID implanted microchips in their bodies.

These technologies allow the possibility of monitoring every single behavior, all the time and everywhere, with the help of surveillance cameras, which are equipped with speakers, so that in the future they may be able to give orders as well.

TransHumanism will bring a new era of slavery to the still very infantile humanity.

While people keep saying, "I can't change the world", or "I can't do anything about it", they will be moving towards an authoritarian, ruthless and monolithic society, without freedom or free will, a world in which these questions will vanish, because the possibility to monitor thoughts will make it impossible to even question or think whatsoever.

These will truly be dark ages for mankind, as humans won't have the possibility to choose between being or not responsible for their spirituality anymore.

The common misuse of responsibility already leads many to magnetic states that influence their emotions and environment, changing their life in a negative direction. And by being aware of this, the Power Elite has been trying to condition humanity to feel constant fear, with economic depressions and war, so that their agenda may be more quickly applied.

Fear is the worse condition in our spiritual path. "The inner fear of yielding to emotion — fear being saturnine in effect and twin sister to worry — seems to require a shock that will take the person so affected out of his environment and set him down in a new place among new conditions before the old conditions can be overcome (Max Heindel, Rosicrucian Fellowship).

We are not who we think we are, but who we haven't chosen to be, because we believe to have a personality reflecting our identity.

Our true identity can only be found in our spirit, but its manifestation is trapped between thoughts, and the lower (as in negative) the frequency of our brainwaves, the more thoughts we have.

Thoughts are a consequence of energy under effect, while the absence of thoughts is the result of energy used for creation.

Although we may justify our actions with our personality, our lack of responsibility and awareness of our personality, and how it is affected by the magnetic field around us, conditions our behaviors and habits.

If you ask an artist what inspiration is, he will tell you that it is manifested when working without the awareness of self, time, space and reason. This condition occurs because creativity is manifested under the influence of theta and delta brainwaves.

Amadeus Mozart (Freemason) knew this well, as he intentionally and subliminally mentioned when writing: "I am a vulgar man! But I assure you, my music is not."

Creativity — or the ability to have positive and uplifting ideas — can be achieved by decreasing the speed of our brainwaves and then keeping a delta state of mind.

This can be practiced when we connect to the magnetic field of the planet, under meditation or other similar exercises.

A few examples on how to do this are walking barefooted or hugging a tree, which produce immediate results, and even faster and easier than meditation, as it is quite difficult to meditate when most of your neighbors are keeping their Wi-Fi devices on, or while being among your own electric devices inside the house.

We must seek for a closer relationship with nature.

Another good strategy to rebalance brainwaves, even though just momentarily, is music and, more precisely, songs that are closer to delta waves of sound, such as classical music, which usually has a speed around 60bmp, the same of a normal heartbeat.

When your heart and mind are synchronized with tranquilizing brainwaves, your own analytical ability improves and you become more effective.

It is delusional to believe that fear and stress are good motivators for energy as education have conditioned the masses to think. "Everything in creation is governed by the law of love" (Antonio Terrer Hernández, Rosicrucian Fellowship).

We live in a world in which physical speed seems more important, but most people go nowhere in life. On the other hand, while highly spiritual individuals seem to be slower than the average, they actually change much faster and obtain faster results than anyone else. This happens because they're connected to the earth's electromagnetic field and more aware of their spiritual needs than others.

You don't need to go faster in life, but merely be in the here and now, for a thought is faster than action, and a good thought can determine which actions increase your results.

Chapter 77: Why Thoughts Differentiate Potential.

You would think that people disagree with you because they have a different viewpoint, but if you knew as much as I do, you would eventually come to the conclusion that the vast majority of the population is mentally ill.

A person who can think, and knows how to get results, independently of his or her background, will always agree with someone else who is also obtaining results in life.

That is why, whenever I find an entrepreneur, we agree on everything we talk, even if we have no clue whatsoever of how any of us does what he does.

You see, the poor focus on tasks, while the rich focus on strategies. But being rich or poor is not related to money. It is related to potential. It is the poor who systematically value potential through money, because they have no clue on how to evaluate potential in any other way.

In medieval times, the rich used to sit on horses back behind a line of soldiers, and the stupid where sent to the battlefield first with their farming tools. It is because they were stupid that they always agreed on this strategy, which often led them to their own death.

The same is applied now when they get a job. Most people are so obsessed with their salary, that they don't even realize that, what they do, has to be, at the very least, three times more profitable for the employer. They literally work for their own pay.

That, as I came to realize, is a reality the poor can't comprehend. And yet, the poor systematically judge you by your income. They have no clue of what money means. And worse than that, they don't know how to evaluate others. They don't value anyone that has potential, because they don't know what that is. What they value is a reflection of themselves: Submission, compliance, obedience, and blind trust.

The poor systematically also make poor choices: They associate with untrustworthy people, they listen to dumb advice, and they copy stupid ideas.

They also get offended by the differentiation between poor and rich, because they think human qualities are related to money. And by acting like this, they keep themselves where they are. For you can't attract that which you are against. And when you oppose wealth, you are not really opposing wealth, but in truth opposing the things that lead to wealth: Intelligence, hard work, trust, values, research (as in seeking for knowledge and being self-educated), commitment, etc.

We may not be responsible for the situation in which we are born, our economic condition, our culture, language and country. But we are surely the ones who keep ourselves there.

The struggle may be hard when you are born without opportunities, but that doesn't mean you can't find them, if you seek them with the right attitude of mind.

The right attitude of mind will lead you to the right people, and such people will give you the opportunities you need, if you know how to behave.

In short, if you have potential, you will never be able to make friends with the stupid and the poor. The stupid and the poor always mock and ridicule what they can't understand. But you don't have to believe me. Just try for yourself and see!

I don't differentiate or discriminate people. They do it to themselves! Their life is a representation of their own thinking.

As a teacher, one of the things that always confused my students, was that I would rather focus on potential than techniques. I was more concerned with teaching the students to think effectively, rather than in their knowing of certain things. And obviously, many resented that.

Their focus was in the results. As a consequence, those ended up with jobs they hate.

It was the ones, who paid attention to what I was doing, and followed my guidelines, that either ended up with the job of their dream, or as business owners. Because, in truth, only potential makes the difference in life.

If you don't know how to think, what you know is of little value.

Chapter 78: The Willingness to Learn.

If I could simplify what I know in three words only, I would say that what makes people different is the willingness to learn.

Unless you are willing to ask questions, listen and admit you have plenty to learn, you are probably part of the idiots.

A change in outcome would have to start in a shift in your awareness, and towards seeing this.

Once you do, others will notice, and then everything I wrote here will present itself as a prophecy.

Quite a lot of people in my life have asked me how can I predict the future so accurately. But I usually don't! I just know that people are predictable. Once you know how they think, you can write a book about their future, wait ten years, and then see them going towards the story you wrote. And yes, I have done this too. I was always right. They always ended as I predicted.

You can even understand the struggles in the past of someone, by analyzing their thinking patterns and beliefs.

I once met a moron that said statistics and research are useless, because only action leads you to results. He also said Universities waste their money in useless studies.

That is like paddling on a boat with holes in it, while being blindfolded.

A lot of people are so stupid, that they truly believe this is the way to live. No wonder his wife abandoned him and took the kids with her. I am even surprised he got married.

Even though I don't discriminate people based on nationalities, if people from Ukraine think like him, it does explain a lot of the situation in that nation.

After saying this, and a bunch of other idiotic nonsense, he asked me if we could meet again.

Taking into consideration I was a college lecturer, and base my entire work, for more than twenty years, in business and books, in extensive research, that is like paddling on a boat full of holes while blindfolded, hit a rock, complain to a farmer nearby about that rock, and then ask if he can get some potatoes next time.

You can't respect that which you can't understand, and you can't understand what you don't know. As a result, the stupid keep themselves stupid, when they are unable to show respect for people they can't comprehend.

The problem then is that, as the poor are often stupid as well, by not being able to learn, they can't accumulate the knowledge that leads them to wealth.

They won't respect the people, the opinions and the opportunities that appear in their life.

The most stupid things that the poor always ask me is:

- "What do you do?"
- "What do you sell?"
- "How do you sell?"
- "How do you advertise?"

They go round and around the same questions, because they only see action. They cannot see strategy.

Their mind is unable to attain that which is abstract. Their conclusions are made based on what is visible. And because of that, they are never able to understand how I make money, even if I openly and honestly answer their questions.

Chapter 79: What Economy Teaches About Society.

We often say or listen to things like,...

- "Don't write books because it doesn't pay well";
- "Don't paint because it doesn't pay well";
- "Don't be a musician because it doesn't pay well".

It's all about don't, don't, don't, because, because, because. And this "because" is always about money. "Virtue has never been as respectable as money" (Mark Twain, Freemason).

"Today almost any person has a present time problem, growing more pressing as time goes on and as our society evolves" (Ron Hubbard, Scientology). But, both the problems and suggestions we hear, are interconnected in the same paradigm. And our thoughts are the result of our paradigms.

These things that individuals, living outside the common paradigm, listen to, are formed under observation, which is limited by life experience. So what the social paradigm really shows, is a majority of shared ideas, a common belief.

You and everyone you know had their dreams crushed by false beliefs, seen often too late to recover years of mistakes, because the educational and social structure are well-built to stop dreamers — creators of alternative realities.

This happens because the Power Elite understands the meaning of inspired creativity as not being merely a gift, as we're told to perceive it, but an inspired act compared to the act of a prophet, that once acted upon can create a chain of changes in the physical world.

When this happens, either the artist is put out of the scene or his art is maintained under the laws of these societies.

That is why, while many musicians end up working for the Power Elite, others are jailed with false accusations or murdered. But it is also for this reason that the Vatican has the biggest art collection in the world.

If we take a closer look at certain laws, we will be able to perceive these common paradigms from a new viewpoint.

As an example, we have the economical principle of Pareto, that states that 80% of the effects in our life come from 20% of the causes. Meaning that, your money comes from 20% of the 80% of your investments.

Some experts in economy say that, if you take the income of your five closest friends, those with whom you spend most of your time with, your income will be within 10% of the average. Which basically means that, you have the average of your five best friends.

We can then conclude that, if your investment increases, so do your own results, or income. "Nothing can stop the man with the right mental attitude from achieving his goal" (Thomas Jefferson, Rosicrucian Fellowship).

This means that faith, determinism, persistence and hard work, when combined, do pay off.

On the other hand, community surveys estimate that, as many as 30% of the adult population in the United States, suffers from mental disorders, which means that 30% of your friends are likely to have mental disorders.

Choosing your friends wisely, can and will determine your future. But if 30% of our closest friends are probably suffering from some kind of mental disorder, 30% of the advices you hear are not worth listening.

Quite often, people think about each other as a reflection of what surrounds them and how they interpret it, but not necessarily as the truth. As a matter of fact, if 30% of the people are mentally ill, 30% of that truth is definitely being misinterpreted.

That is a lot, more precisely, 25% of what you hear; at least 25% of what you hear is not true.

Now, here you are, investing 80% of your time in people who are probably mentally ill and have no idea of what they are talking about. How can you be successful?

Obviously, nothing of what they say matters. It matters only what you do:

- What you spend your time doing, but also how fast and how much you do it;

- The people you associate yourself with and your capacity to differentiate them.

If you spend a vast amount of time studying the strategies to reach your goals, and seeking for opportunities to meet the people who can lead you there, by their way of thinking or life experience, you are more likely to get what you want, whatever it is.

Then, as me, you will accomplish what others consider to be impossible. And they won't believe what for you is a reality.

You may share your life with them, but it would be like two people from different realities sharing the same space.

I have been in relationships in which the person living with me, could not believe what I do. She would see it and not really understand. Basically, the person that she was with wasn't me. It was someone inside her own imaginary.

It may be shocking to realize and affirm that most people are mentally ill. It isn't just an observation, but truly part of an experience that affects us. Because, I must say, it feels very strange to realize that you spent, sometimes years, next to someone who never really saw you.

That person fabricated an idea of you that was never there. The gap between your identity and the individual in her head, can be so wide, that you wonder how both of you were able to communicate.

Chapter 80: The Impact of Our Social Paradigms.

We learn almost everything we know as a group, inside the family, school, and later as employees and pawns, within a multitude of events related to work and relationships.

As a consequence, our paradigms are formed under the idea of 'I can't do it alone'. But "If you can't live alone, you were born a slave" (Fernando Pessoa, Rosicrucian Fellowship).

It wasn't a common paradigm, a social group or even a country, that changed the world, but individuals. And that is why our problems can be resumed to the same mind programming, the paradigms that condition our thoughts and decisions throughout our life, as well as our interactions with others.

Many may have studied the same subject, or created different theories and perspectives about it, but one individual only took action and manifested the...

- Car — Karl Benz;

- Light bulb — Thomas Edison;

- Fax machine — Jerome Lemelson.

- Radio transmission — Guglielmo Marconi;

Free minds change the world, not groups of people.

Our environment and its objects, money included, are just tools that we use to reach our goals, not the path itself. And should never be confused with the ultimate purpose, which is enlightenment.

Within this insight, there's also the fact that most people, unaware of this knowledge and irresponsible about their spiritual evolution, living an animalistic state of mind conditioned by their emotions, are just tools and not fit to be creators, leaders or even friends, and should never be trusted for this same reason.

Even when using the tools of others, what the masses do, is behave as tools of a system, by doing what they've been programmed to do, instead of thinking by themselves. And this is why "if you're explaining, you're losing" (Ronald E. Reagan, Knights of Malta).

The value of a tool is measured by its predictability, and that's how we evaluate good workers in any position of the social hierarchy. But this doesn't mean that those that believe in the system are trustable as individuals. They are many times the most disgusting of all human beings, because they're willing to die and kill to protect a lie.

"When a man assumes a public trust he should consider himself a public property" (Thomas Jefferson, Rosicrucian Fellowship).

We must not trust those who can't trust themselves.

The real evil force that we must always oppose, is manifested in those that blindly obey the rulers of the delusional world, namely, soldiers, politicians, police officers, teachers, physicians, nurses, dentists, psychologists and psychiatrists. Because, "a thing which is always subject to the direction of another is somewhat of a dead thing" (Thomas Aquinas, Catholic Priest and member of the Rosicrucian Fellowship).

The exceptions in these groups are minorities, and difficult to find, as most end up losing their jobs when speaking and acting in defense of the truth.

It's difficult to post a threat to the system of things as we know it today, because most of the leaders occupying key positions in the world, and in many important institutions, have been carefully selected by their loyalty and not wisdom.

It's more important how people perceive themselves inside the system than what they think about who they are.

People can't really help anyone by saying "you should" or "you shouldn't", but they do help when providing the necessary tools to achieve your dreams, or when being themselves a tool to help you. And that's the moment when you realize their real value.

"The holy passion of Friendship is of so sweet and steady and loyal and enduring a nature, that it will last through a whole lifetime, if not asked to lend money" (Mark Twain, Freemason).

It may be difficult to make money with writing, painting, photography, or any other form of art, but many people can, and there are many paths to achieve it, even though two changes are always the most significant in this process: yourself and your reality.

You must change yourself or your reality. Because, despite what we've been taught to believe, "the solution and possibilities to solve a problem are many" (Vladimir Putin, Freemason).

Chapter 81: Perspective and Relativity.

When I wrote my first book, everyone said I wouldn't make much money as an author and should stop writing.

Their conclusion was based in the total amount of revenue I made from that book — a 700 pages book on education that sold zero copies.

After writing more than 300 books, and reaching the Amazon, Kobo and Apple bestselling charts more than 100 times, and with different titles, my income increased dramatically, allowing me to travel the world, and never need another job again.

A common person wouldn't even write 10 books in 4 years, or in a lifetime, but that is the element of individuality in action, and that's why we can't judge our dream, or judge others based on our background.

"This dream, like the winged messenger, seems to be divinely inspired and hints at the opportunity that is about to present itself" (Soror E.A.S., Rosicrucian Fellowship).

We dream about what we can achieve, but others judge according to what they can see. And all they see is a person holding to something that they interpret with their own mind.

In truth, they know nothing about that individual's potential and, very often, even the individual himself isn't aware of it; not until he puts himself to the test.

Most people project themselves in what they see, so they judge others based on their self-judgments of "I can't, therefore, you can't". But judgments are merely projections of personal paradigms.

"We think too small, like the frog at the bottom of the well. He thinks the sky is only as big as the top of the well, but if he surfaced, he would have an entirely different view" (Mao Zedong).

Every physically orientated goal is an illusion, including money. It is never about what you see, but what you can do with what is seen, and it is never about wealth, but what you can do when having it.

"Instinct of love toward an object demands a mastery to obtain it" (Sigmund Freud, Freemason).

Interestingly, just like the paradigm is shaped by the mind with the information received by the environment, people change their attitude in the same way. "If a person feels they can't control the object or feel threatened by it, they act negatively toward it" (Sigmund Freud, Freemason).

Those that refuse to change their paradigm, and adjust to your achievements, will leave your life if you succeed, and eventually abandon you. One day, you'll simply stop receiving their replies.

They will create all kind of excuses to justify their unreasonable behavior, the unseen insanity. But "fame must have enemies, as light must have gnats. Do no bother yourself about it; disdain. Keep your mind serene as you keep your life clear" (Victor Hugo, Rosicrucian Fellowship).

Those willing to change their paradigm, will shift from,..

- "You can't make money from...";
- "You can't make significant amounts from...";
- "You can't make a living from...";

To finally say,...

- "I knew you could make it".

This is why what we think about ourselves is more important than what others make us believe.

As an example of this, notice that Tom Cruise (winner of three Global Globe Awards, and Scientologist), said: "As a young actor, people were trying to define who I was before I really knew that for myself. But I still remember thinking, 'This is what I love doing, and I hope I'm going to be able to do it forever'".

We must be honest with our true self, and above common beliefs in regarding to who we are or should be. For the raw truth is that real friends are only those that dream with you.

Others are enemies of your spiritual achievements and you mustn't share anything with them, not even your dreams or thoughts.

Your power in life comes when you realize how the social belief system works. This will allow you to reposition yourself on the spectrum of life and restart a new karmic wheel of experiences.

"We can't have full knowledge all at once. We must start by believing; then afterwards we may be led on to master the evidence for ourselves" (Thomas Aquinas, Catholic Priest and member of the Rosicrucian Fellowship).

Solving problems isn't about closing your eyes to them, but facing them with the necessary available information.

This confrontation may lead to suffering and regret, but "the emotion of remorse cleanses and purifies the desire body of weeds and tares, leaving the soil free and fostering for the growth of manifold virtues, that blossom into spiritual advancement and bring greater opportunities for service in the Master's vineyard" (Max Heindel, Rosicrucian Fellowship).

This truth can be resumed by the fact that human beings are measured by the amplitude and commitment to their dreams. "A seed is useless and impotent unless it is put in its appropriate matrix" (Christian Rosenkreuz, Rosicrucian Fellowship).

Chapter 82: Most People Will Die With Their Dreams.

Human beings have an egotistic need to be correct all the time, and that is what makes it difficult to accept any change in their reality. To be wrong is a contradiction to the self, reason why most people can't find their life purpose, as who they are, and what they should be doing, is spiritually related.

These individuals are living in denial, because they can't accept the fact that, family, life, happiness, money, career, love, and even power, aren't forever. And above everything, they have a tremendous difficulty in accepting that they don't own anything or anybody, although attachments in this lifetime made them believe they do.

You can't control the future, events or people, but you can understand them to increase the probability of success. This is why, while the majority wishes to predict the future to know what's going to happen, the Power Elite does it to change what will happen.

While most people neglect the need to make plans and organize their life, in order to have a better future, the Power Elite plans the future, not only for this generation, but for the next.

We may want to believe that previous world wars and economic depressions have awakened people from their deep sleep, but they didn't, and that's why history keeps repeating itself.

In 2020, governments from all over the world, where able to force people into locking themselves at home, with the excuse of a virus. In some of these countries, laws were passed to enforce vaccination on the population.

Despite the fact that many laws were debated, it became obvious that the population of the world is submissive and never questions authority.

This situation made it obvious that it would be as easy to murder them now as it was during the Holocaust.

Another thing that was obvious, was how easy it is to control public opinion, for most people are too stupid to think for themselves. They will believe anything they are told.

People want to be right, but if you are wrong believing that you are right, life will make you realize this within your mind, heart and soul — that's the source of psychosomatic illnesses.

"Illusions commend themselves to us because they save us pain and allow us to enjoy pleasure instead. We must therefore accept it without complaint when they sometimes collide with a bit of reality against which they are dashed to pieces" (Sigmund Freud, Freemason).

The truth is that your personal beliefs aren't important to anyone else, unless they can use them for their own personal benefit. "Only aim to do your duty, and mankind will give you credit where you fail" (Thomas Jefferson, Rosicrucian Fellowship).

As you develop your awareness, you must recognize that, without the fundamental knowledge of the gnostic truths, necessary to your spiritual freedom, you are nothing more that a social element created from a multitude of events that contributed to your personality, as well as your potential.

In order to increase this potential, you must change your personality, for only you are responsible for your own reality.

Chapter 83: Wealth is Always Relative to Location.

Let us consider the amount of US $500 in 2020. It may not be much if you live in the United States, Germany, or Switzerland, but more than one billion people — one-sixth of the world's population — lives in extreme poverty, on less than one dollar a day.

The average monthly income in Belarus (Europe) is around $200, although people still manage to pay food, flats and smartphones. In Belarus Universities, Lecturers working full-time earn less than shop assistants, around $197 per month. But in China, the most powerful economy in the world, a college lecturer earns an average of 500 dollars a month.

In Portugal (Europe), $700 is the minimum wage. But while in most European countries, is impossible to rent an apartment for this amount of money, in Ireland and the south of Spain, you can rent a room for half of that ($350). And, for the same quantity, you can rent a whole house in the north of Portugal, with three rooms and a living room.

If we extend this analysis to a yearly income, consider that, working during two years for the minimum wage in Australia, Luxembourg, Monaco, San Marino, New Zealand, Belgium and the Netherlands, allows you to buy an apartment with ocean view in the touristic south of Portugal or Spain.

In other words, someone working as a barista in Australia, has a better chance of buying her freedom in two years, than most residents in the European peninsula have in twenty.

Reality is indeed only an illusion. The more you feed your mind with information like the one that was just now provided, the easier it becomes to make plans for the future and dream. And that is why knowledge is potential power, in the sense that, the more you know, the more you can do with your life.

I also found interesting to notice that, the cheapest places to live in the world are, at the same time, some of the most beautiful, and often chosen merely for tourism, such as Thailand, the Philippines and Malaysia.

In Thailand, for example, near the coast, and in 2020, a room in an apartment runs at roughly $90 upwards. But I have lived in a hotel room in Thailand, with view to the mountains, plenty of sunshine during the day, a king size bed, television, and a big swimming pool included, for only $150 a month; and paid no more than one dollar a day to eat a good meal in local restaurants.

As for the efforts that most people put in having and keeping a job that provides them a good income, I must say that you're not as rich as the amount of money you make, but the amount you can keep after spending what you earn.

To illustrate this explanation, is suffice to say that, while a manager in many countries, including Singapore, Hong Kong and China, can earn between US $1000 to $5000, an employee of McDonalds in Sweden, a bartender in Luxembourg, and a taxi driver in Australia can earn the same. But the minimum wage in Switzerland, in 2020, is above $6000, which means you can earn that by cleaning toilets as well.

In the world we live today, freedom can also be more expensive than the lack of it, and to prove it we have the prisons of Sweden, which offer better conditions than any slum house of Brazil.

Chapter 84: Love or Money?

Freedom, careers, income and housing, are related to the perception of wealth that leads many people to value or devalue themselves according to what they possess. And indeed, the value of a human life has decreased so much in the latest centuries, that by 2010 was possible to legally buy, a young, beautiful and virgin Vietnamese wife for only $5000. And aren't women in other countries for sale too?

I have never met one woman in Europe that has asked me what I studied in college, or what my work experience is. Their questions are all related to money.

Many may disagree with me on this, but,…

- "I am looking for a man with a good job", is related to money;

- "I am looking for a man with a good house", is related to money;

- "I want a man with a good car", is related to money;

- "I want a man who takes me on vacations around the world", is related to money;

- "I want a man that takes me to fancy restaurants all the time", is related to money;

- "I want a man that buys me expensive gifts", is related to money.

We could argue that women actually want security and not money, but can you feel safe without money?

You can't! Money pays for everything, including security guards, guns and Rottweilers, if you need to expand on your own safety.

The more materialistic a society is, the less spiritual value it has. For everyone starts chasing social validation, which completely nullifies the importance of other characteristics within the human spectrum.

"I went on your social media profile and saw that you write books, so I bought one to understand you better", said no woman ever. But they do say,...

- "I saw that you travel", which is related to her need for validation;

- "I saw that you have many friends", which is related to her need for validation;

- "I saw that you are famous", which is related to her need for validation.

These superficial aspects have everything to do with selfish and narcissistic needs, and nothing to do with the character of a person.

Many would say: — "Men are like that too!", And I agree. But if someone says that there are exceptions, I would say that this person has not experienced life as much as I did.

As soon as you start meeting people by the thousands, you quickly lose your childish sense of perception of the world. And then you realize that normal is the exception.

Most people are not normal. They even relativize normal, so that you may not realize how abnormal they are.

Chapter 85: Absurd Facts About Money.

Money has nothing to do with moral.

As strange and insulting as it may seem, money reveals our true nature.

It is not correct to say that money is evil, because money is an object. It would be like saying that a gun is evil, or a rock is evil, or the air is evil.

Objects don't possess human attributes. People do!

What you can understand about money, has everything to do with people, and nothing with money.

The more you understand people, the richer you will be. But this world is made by people. So what can you assimilate from this reality?

- If you're willing to clean toilets for one year in a rich country, you can buy a house in a beautiful place and own a beautiful woman, while being surrounded by old and retired British and North Americans, that spent an entire lifetime working to achieve the same, and only have about 10 to 15 years left in their existence, to enjoy the same before they die.

- As a woman, you can't really find a very rich guy that easily, unless you are willing to sleep with many until you find one.

- As a man, you can't find a proper wife, unless you have enough money.

In both cases — for men and women, money becomes irrelevant if, either they don't need social validation, or they don't value themselves high enough.

I haven't cleaned toilets or bough any of the beautiful women I have lived with, but I have no doubt that many of them wanted to be with me because of my money and the opportunity of traveling with me.

It is also obvious, by the eyes of the people I encounter all over the planet, that they hate me. Why wouldn't they? I have what they want! I have the freedom they may never have!

They don't care how much I worked to get this lifestyle. In fact, zero persons have asked me how hard it is to get what I have. They all ask questions related to shortcuts, as if I had a magic formula to making money.

You will never find a book like this one in your life. It resumes the best knowledge on the topic. But do you think they will read it? No! They will just try to make me resume these pages in a ten minutes conversation. That's how imbecile they are!

I often end up spending more on drinks and food with these morons than they would spend on this book. They do deserve their misery!

At least, in countries like the Philippines, India, and Brazil, if I put this book for free, thousands of people will download it in the first week. The rest of the world couldn't care less.

In some cases, like England, I will probably be insulted for offering the book. They will say it's a worthless book and that is why it is free. Because when you offer something of a tremendous value to worthless people, that's what you get in return — insults.

In the eyes of many, I have cheated on the game of life. They are unaware that their whole existence was a lie and they were the ones who got cheated. But one "can't be himself without being willing to grant beingness, because he's the only one that can grant beingness to himself" (Ron Hubbard, Scientology).

Wealth is an illusion determined only by conceptualizations about it. And naturally, if I don't feel good in any country, I keep on traveling.

There are about 200 countries on the entire planet, and I haven't visited half yet. If I change country every year, I still can't see them all, unless I live up to 200 years of age.

I travel, but I also work, and a lot. But if you don't want to work a single day again in your life, the solution can be as simple as renting a new house, or using the house bought by your grandfather, and then making spare rooms available to tourists.

That is what many young Italians and Spanish are doing. If you own a house in cities life Florence or Barcelona, European history and touristic propaganda, will bring the money to you.

Chapter 86: The Alchemical Transmutation.

The stages of transmutation are the same for everyone, and they also apply for gaining wealth. I will use my own example to illustrate them. For those that knew I was a writer, kept telling me:

— "You can't make a living as a writer!", Because they were measuring the activity by its results.

This is something that education teaches us to do, and that is why people tend to have difficulties in seeing the world from other perspectives that aren't related to results, appreciation or wealth.

They forget that these elements are superficial to life and you can't really control them.

The paradigm shows itself along the whole process of confronting others with something they analyze based on this assessment. And so, before becoming an author, I was facing laughter, ridicule and disdain, when mentioning that I wanted to become one, because my background and achievements were related to music, not words.

"You may have to fight when there is no hope of victory, because it is better to perish than to live as slaves" (Winston Churchill, Freemason and member of the Ancient Order of Druids of Oxford).

You have to look at your life purpose, what you love to do, and your ability to learn from your mistakes, while correcting your actions, to fulfill yourself in this life.

Such attitude is more important than the results or the recognition of others, because it will allow you to gain control over those same results and permanently change your life.

"Change will not come if we wait for some other person or some other time. We are the ones we've been waiting for. We are the change that we seek" (Barack Obama, Martinist Order).

In this process, even if you are just dealing with plans and methods, there is a huge amount of self-awareness to be exercised, developed and recognized.

In my case, I already knew that I love to create things in the field of art, either as a designer or a musician. I just didn't know how to transform these passions into a business.

The first opportunity to do that, came from music, when I started organizing events and hiring DJs. And although the results were very positive, they always redirected me to another experience, that I wasn't seeing before, related to sharing my knowledge in a creative way.

Within this reality, the correlation between music, teaching and writing was obvious, because I was never looking at music or teaching as a process in itself, but instead the connections between me and others, the emotions transmitted, and the way I could express them better.

The sense of fulfillment made me become aware that this was the path, not the end to my journey.

I then started using the same skills to take my entire knowledge one step ahead, and that was writing books.

The feeling that I was within my life purpose, and loving this new activity, was so obvious, that I wasn't bothered by spending an average of sixteen hours a day, seven days a week, writing, and for many years of my life, one book after another, without any break.

It was so natural for me to do this, if someone had asked me to stop, it would be like asking me to stop breathing; and I would prefer to write when sick, than to stop writing and be in bed, for I would feel much worse.

Chapter 87: What Happens When You Surrender to God?

When I found my path in this life, I didn't have to worry about the rest. Constant job offers, and dozens of them, would fall into my email box without any request or search, especially when I needed them the most.

I also received many offers from friends to be their partner in business and start businesses with them. And even the bank offered me money when I needed it the most, which I used to travel and work abroad for a better schedule, in order to have much more free time to write books.

It was as if God was acknowledging my efforts in working for him and uplifting mankind with what I know, so I never have to worry about money. "God truly loves those who fight in solid lines for His cause, like a well-compacted wall" (Solid Lines, In The Quran).

After two years writing books, I found the job and life that any writer could wish. I was working only two hours a week as a lecturer, living for free in a huge hotel apartment with everything, including a big kitchen, had four months of paid vacations a year, which meant not having those two working hours during 1/3 of the year, and dated some of the most beautiful women I ever met in my life. Because although I did not have the motivation to date anyone, women would approach me in the coffee shops were I was working, which also allowed me to make lots of friends and meet many interesting people.

This represented a huge change in my lifestyle, because just four years before that, I was working very hard, seven days a week, with one full-time job as manager of a multinational training company, three businesses in the music industry and 4 part-time jobs related to teaching and sports instruction.

I was sleeping an average of three hours a day, in order to find time between eleven o'clock at night, when I arrived home from a very busy day, and two in the morning, the moment when I couldn't keep my eyes open, to continue writing my first books.

I never had to plan what to write and I never calculated the amount of money I can make with books. Since I started writing, God has put in my life more experiences, knowledge and interesting people than what I can describe in my writings.

Due to this overflow of ideas and inspiration, I was able to write faster than what I could publish, and therefore, although only about a few hundreds of my books are available to the public, I have written a lot more about many different topics.

God provides everything I need, and I'm now a full-time writer that travels the world.

I have accomplished everything with faith, persistence and hard work, although it seems that most people can't accept this explanation for success. But "to one who has faith, no explanation is necessary, and to one without faith, no explanation is possible" (Thomas Aquinas, Catholic Priest and member of the Rosicrucian Fellowship).

Today, "I am at peace with God. My conflict is with Man" (Charlie Chaplin, Loyal Order of Moose). Because, wherever I go, people look at me as if I was an insult to their existence.

Chapter 88: Haters Will Hate!

It doesn't matter how nice or friendly and helpful I am to other people, because they will always hate me for being better than them in some way.

The reasons for this hate, as I have found, and despite my surprise every time it happens, are always the same:

- I look 10 to 15 years younger than I really am;
- I can work when I want, and stop working when I want too;
- I can earn my money — which is passive income — as I sleep.

Jealousy is difficult to tolerate for too long. Most people make me feel uncomfortable, also because they think I must be doing something illegal.

At the very least, they could wonder if I am descendant of monarchs, which would be a fact, but they never do. They think I a member of some criminal organization.

Many have actually reported me to the police, because, I am probably so confident that it scares them. And I travel so much, that I am always stopped in some airport, and checked for drugs.

However, the strong criticism often comes from those who are themselves members of a religion. They think it's impossible for someone to write so much. They think their Holy books belong to some parallel reality where authors live.

For some mysterious reason, they don't value the authors in front of them.

The attitude of fellow authors and even readers also affects me, as when they report my books, and such books are then removed from different platforms for investigation, and usually when they are selling the most.

I have to then wait months for these investigations to finish, and get the book back into the platform.

Sadly, most readers are also too stupid for what I write. They can't see the value. And then insult in their reviews, saying that I just copy a bunch of quotes.

These morons don't know what is a research. And apparently, think my content is inferior to someone that says whatever comes to his head, without any life experience or proper investigation.

Most people actually think anyone can write one of my books.

That will never happen in the next three thousand years, but they have no clue even of how real knowledge is produced.

When that isn't enough, they turn to my personal life, without any idea whatsoever of the vast amount of things I did before, or how significant they were.

They also disregard the amount of time and efforts necessary to create a book like this one.

The masses are a lot much dumber and cruel than I thought they were. That's why I have divided myself in many different pen-names.

The biggest challenge, from what I came to understand, comes from people trying to stop us. Apart from this, there is no challenge greater enough to defeat an inspired person.

"Blessed are those who are persecuted for righteousness' sake, for theirs is the kingdom of heaven" (Matthew 5:10).

Chapter 89: God is Your Best Companion.

I would never go so far in life without God guiding my way.

With the help of God, it only took me about five years to finally reach the life I once dreamed about but thought to be impossible to achieve.

I can't precisely describe how I got here, because the steps combine a huge amount of unpredictable situations and events, that nobody could describe with detail in a book.

Certainly, it wouldn't be possible without faith and love for what I do, and that's the glue connecting the pieces of both small and big experiences, from the heaviest in difficulty to the lightest in beauty.

I do need to have plenty of love, to share amazing knowledge that has changed my life and the life of people I met, and helped, with the rest of the world, as I then see part of this same world showing depreciation, by writing hateful and cruel reviews about such books, and while another part keeps silent.

It would be easier if more people gave me good reviews, to encourage the efforts and show a belief in the work, but that is part of the challenge you'll also face in your life, as I saw it many times in other people's life as well.

More importantly, I have lots of fun with my work, because I usually write in coffee shops, sometimes with friends from many countries around me, including France, Germany, India, United States, Spain, Saudi Arabia, Russia, Venezuela, China and others, sharing their life experiences and thoughts, and inspiring my writing with their energy.

Luckily for me, the most beautiful places in the world tend to have the kindest, wisest and friendliest people as well.

From another perspective, I may not yet be successful and never will be in the eyes of my family, that expect me to make thousands of dollars a month working in an office in some North American or European Company. I may also not be successful in the eyes of my students, which would expect me to continue working as a lecturer in a big city and a famous university. But I am successful to myself, because I have conquered the beautiful lifestyle I always dreamed about during my entire life. I am a full-time artist in my own paradise and I couldn't be happier for achieving this goal.

The day I entered an uninhabited island in the Philippines, it was like I was entering inside the wallpaper that I had in the screen of my computer for many years, when I was still a student, to inspire me to dream. At that moment, I was inside my dream.

That was an alchemical transmutation that I have experienced countless times, because with success also comes the understanding of how to be successful. But it was only the first step of my journey, as I realized that this wasn't the country I had chosen to live as a writer, and decided to continue chasing my biggest dream, instead of succumbing to the reality or a partially accomplished dream.

To be more precise, I live with the constant conscience of three realities:

- The material world;

- My emotional world;

- My mental world.

But I don't worry much about the first, because the Kingdom of God, that Jesus talked about, is in the other two, and these are the most important.

If you want the same for yourself, "seek first the kingdom of God and his righteousness, and all these things will be added to you" (Matthew 6:33, in The Bible). "God will be enough for those who put their trust in Him" (Divorce, In The Quran).

Chapter 90: The Path of Self-Destruction.

I have accomplished many things that are seen as impossible and unreal for everyone around me, and yet, the fact remains that I have truly done it.

With this transmutation, I have also gained many spiritual powers, which I stopped describing to others, because first they ridicule and doubt, but when shown, they fear it and fear me.

The world isn't ready for many things, so there will always be secrets that we must keep to avoid mass paranoia while developing ourselves in the light of God.

You too will gain many special powers that you thought to be impossible to exist, by following the knowledge in this book.

You don't need to fear those abilities, and they have nothing to do with demonic possession, as many unintelligent and uninformed individuals believe.

"Individuality is only possible if it unfolds from wholeness", so there's actually "more sense in our nonsense and more nonsense in our sense" (David Bohm, Physicist).

Spiritual powers are gifts from God, for proving yourself honest and trustworthy in your faith, and for your endeavors in the path towards the light. They are as natural as your journey in life as a spirit.

In this world, demonic possession is reserved to those that don't believe that they have a spirit, as well as those that, in their greed and arrogance, reject their own spirituality and moral responsibility towards the rest of mankind.

God allows demonic power over the unfaithful, the untruthful and the cruel, as a path to their self-destruction, just like He closes the mind and heart of those that neglect the path of the light. "Wrongdoers only have each other to protect them; the righteous have God Himself as their protector" (Kneeling, In The Quran).

These will never recognize the truth, they'll always be blind to this truth and the truth won't find them.

They will laugh about the unknown to suppress their fear of what they can't see, and the suffering that such light can cause them, when revealing the darkness in which they live, as well as the pain that will come from the awareness of regret, guilt, sin and remorse. "On the Day when excuses will not profit the evildoers, their fate will be rejection and they will have the worst of homes" (In The Quran 40:39).

Truly, those that hide the most, create their own darkness, because they can only hide the truth from themselves. And even if the truth is revealed to them within their secret societies, it will be reinterpreted in their mind according to their wicked desires.

They may even create a new religious philosophy from what they have learned but it won't have anything to do with the truth. Their words will be rotten fruits from their distorted mind, because God won't water their spirit.

"Alas for those whose hearts harden at the mention of God! They have clearly lost their way" (The Throngs, In The Quran).

Hell is within the wicked and they are already dead without knowing it. If you want to meet Satan, all you need to do is look deep into their eyes. And it is not surprising indeed, that one of the rules for participating in a Bilderberg meeting, the one that gathers the most influential and powerful individuals in the world, is not to look any participant in the eyes.

Nonetheless, crying is for the eyes as sorrow is for the heart. Both are natural cleansing processes. But you'll more likely see a Christian crying than a Banker, because one has indoctrinated himself into the idea of being as a sheep, while the other has educated himself in thinking like a wolf.

Chapter 91: Time and Transmutation.

The amount of time needed to achieve your dreams is relative to many variants, and depends on your own personal path.

"Dreams are the royal road to the unconscious" (Sigmund Freud), and not even you know what is hiding in your subconscious until you reach it.

Maybe some people would say that five years is a lot of time to achieve our dreams, but I prefer to see it from another perspective. I had a friend with 65 years old that was working 7 days a week as a teacher, and can't anymore because she was fired for being too old to work. She spent her entire life believing in the system and now is seen by this same system as an expired package of milk.

For the society, her life ended, but for her it never really begun. And so, although 5 years seems a lot of time, it is more for a 65 year old woman than for a 30 year old man.

The saddest sentence I ever heard, came from a 70 year old painter I met in the United States. She said:

— "My mother died at 75, I'm 70, and I haven't achieved any award with my paintings."

She was looking for a solution and that is why she couldn't find any in me. But she shouldn't be angry when I persuaded her to talk about the negative things happening in the United States, as the basic problem in her dozens of paintings is that they don't transmit any message.

Abstract art painters often spend too much time hiding behind their nonsense, instead of using the freedom that this style in particular allows.

As one critic told her:

— "Any monkey could do the same".

Somehow, he was correct, although there is something worse in the way she paints than in what a monkey would do, and that's the sense of hopelessness, need, fear and despair. The world has enough of that already!

The shortest path to success in art, if I could put it into words, is altruism, but if you don't care about anything in the world, and even get angry at people that show you the truth, how can you be altruistic? And why would you paint, or draw, or even create music, if you're not altruistic?

There is not much we can do for such individuals. "The ego is not master in its own house" (Sigmund Freud, Freemason).

"God leaves whoever He will to stray and guides whoever He will. Do not waste your soul away with regret for them: God knows exactly what they do" (The Creator, In The Quran).

I have achieved my dreams by sacrificing five years of my youth and health, but already have a huge background of life experience behind me.

For most people, even sacrificing merely one year of their life, with intense discipline and hard work, while waking up early in the morning and every morning, seems crazy, and that's why they can't transform their energy and achieve the new reality they want. But "God's promise is true, so do not let the present life deceive you" (The Creator, In The Quran).

The word sacrifice is actually unpleasant for most individuals, but it is the correct word to apply here, as you do need to destroy your previous personality, in order to recreate a new one, that will then match the life you want.

You can't create a new life with the person you once were.

"Human salvation demands the divine disclosure of truths surpassing reason" (Thomas Aquinas, Catholic Priest and member of the Rosicrucian Fellowship).

Chapter 92: Why You Must Serve God.

In a not so distant past, I didn't have any time to go anywhere, and couldn't keep a normal relationship with anyone. But two years later I was sleeping an average of eight hours a day, and having the time and money to travel all over Europe and Asia.

In less than two years, I was in France, Spain, Portugal, Switzerland, Germany, England, Italy, Turkey, China, India, The Philippines, Thailand, Malaysia, Singapore, Hong Kong, Macau, and Indonesia. And also living for a certain period in these countries as a writer, when not lecturing at a university.

I visited some of these countries more than once, because I love Italy and small paradises on Earth like the Philippines.

As for the money that allowed me to travel so much, I can positively say that it came out of nowhere. "My Lord gives in abundance to whoever He will" (So Sheba, In The Quran).

Most people can't see, even if you tell them, that money doesn't exist. Money is literally speaking an IOU – I owe you.

We are all exchanging beliefs between one another.

We live in a planet in which humans believe that, if they give a piece of paper to someone, that someone will do something for them. So we work for pieces of paper.

Then, we use those pieces of paper to buy stuff and food, because the ones that receive our pieces of paper believe that they can also use it for themselves.

"Money is simply a symbol that people are confident can be converted into goods" (Ron Hubbard, Scientology).

If I was giving ILUs (I love you) to people, it would not work, wouldn't it?

If I gave ITUs (I trust you) to people, it would not work as well, right?

As humans, we have learned to love and trust money, while losing love and trust for one another. That is how money became the anti-Christian symbol of our world, opposing the Christian alchemic transmutation as Jesus taught us.

By putting my trust in God and my love in the alchemical transmutation, which working on my dreams led me to, I was able to attract ideas, and those ideas inspired me to create something new.

That which I created was a product with value.

Indeed, "those who submit to God have found wise guidance" (The Jinn, In The Quran).

As I improved the value of my productivity by working on it, I was able to listen more carefully to what God was trying to tell me to do, and that's how you attune to your life purpose on earth. It is like synchronizing to a radio frequency, until you find a clear and non-disruptive signal, which in this case, is the beautiful harmony of the voice of God, speaking from your subconscious, while at the same time, showing correlated signs in the physical world, which you perceive with consciousness.

I never follow anything that isn't correlated between my subconscious and conscious perceptions, as I know that this is how I identify the message that God has for me.

This is also how God protects me, when sending messages about my enemies and my future, far before anyone gains any advantage.

Chapter 93: God Helps Those Who Help Themselves.

I have written many books that otherwise would be impossible, due to messages received in dreams, and I have also predicted future events that would affect my life tremendously, by receiving warnings through the same process.

"Everyone does things their own way, but your Lord is fully aware of who follows the best-guided path" (The Quran 17:72).

Over the years, God has been increasing my salary, which comes from different sources, namely, my own books. And when people, in their greed, try to take it away from me in some way, God shows me new paths.

This is why I don't compete against any human being in what I do.

The constant cycle of ideas I get, are orders received by God, and the people I meet are assignments He gives me, in order to fulfill his tasks. So I keep on trusting Him and, as a consequence, money keeps flowing into my life. And because I'm a good worker, God keeps giving me more projects in the form of ideas, and more challenges as well.

"Do people think they will be left alone after saying 'We believe' without being put to the test?" God "tested those who went before them: God will certainly mark out which ones are truthful and which are lying" (Alif Lam Mint, In The Quran).

The real temple of God is within your heart. And I do my best, by dedicating my whole life and time to Him.

He compensated me, first by allowing me to enjoy vacations in many beautiful countries and work in these countries as well, and then the same without the need to work for anyone else in the countries I choose to live.

If God "created the heavens and the earth and everything in between" (Sad, in The Q'uran), I guess I'm probably spending most of my time in between.

When I sit in a coffee shop, feeling peaceful with the sun in my face, and watching people passing by from point A to point B, and then from point B to A, thinking about work and stressing about bills, I feel like a ghost, not a common human.

In this company that people call life, I don't fear or worry about the future, but many around me can't understand why.

In truth, I know that "the happy ending is awarded to those who are mindful of God" (The Story, In The Quran).

I don't fear the future because I know that, if God fires me from His organization that I call life, and takes away from me my project, which I call life purpose, I can always find another job, working for Satan and paper money, like anyone else.

Whatever is the choice, I can always go back to God's company, because He doesn't send anyone away forever like humans do. He just forces us to learn with the rival, so that humans can then become more efficient in God's company.

Sometimes I try to find people to work for me and help me, as my partners in God's company, but humans don't accept 'I Love Yous' or 'I Trust Yous', and I prefer not to owe anyone anything except to God, and so I don't offer them any 'I Owe Yous' either. Besides, how could I offer 'Owes' to someone that doesn't exchange 'Trusts' and 'Loves' with me?

I can't offer promises to someone that doesn't show love or trust.

The only thing worth working for is love and trust, and you increase your value by being lovable and trustable.

Chapter 94: The Path of Darkness.

If everyone started achieving their dreams with the knowledge presented in this book, the whole system would bankrupt and fail.

That is why movies, the media and TV advertisements, have a huge investment behind them, backing the efforts to make sure that you stay inside the programming that the Power Elite intends to maintain.

With propaganda and "scientific research", it is very easy to do adjustments in that programming along the way.

That is also why we have passports and have to present ourselves as belonging to a certain country and a certain race of people, even though it doesn't make any sense with the huge amount of migration and interbreeding that human history has witnessed.

Unless a person realizes this madness and the prison in which one is living, won't ever be able to wake up and change reality, independently of what he or she might believe. For the world is designed to keep people under certain parameters.

Before becoming a writer and gradually changing my life in a new direction, I had debts that were five times more than my salary, had nearly no social life due to the lack of free time available, and was living under the effects of high amounts of sugar, vitamins and other chemicals to keep me awake during the day and asleep during the night, and had many physical illnesses, as well as an increasing depression that could have killed me faster than anything else. But one day I said to myself: "enough!"

I then decided to quit my jobs and work at night as a security-guard for one year.

During those very cold winters, surrounded by darkness and the smell of feces from the broken toilet near me, I read for 12 hours a day, and pushed my spirit and the laws of the universe as much as I could.

I did that with what I had studied in religious societies throughout my entire life, and by perfecting my awareness during that year, and applying it for the very first time with the intention of changing my future.

Life isn't always perfect, everyone has problems, and the biggest challenge, when we wish to change, may be related to our darkest fears and learning to confront them.

My biggest fear was related to not being important as a person, not having a job that dignifies me, and not having a fulfilling social life. Therefore, this job was perfect to make me feel isolated, humiliated and unimportant to society.

I accepted it and appreciated the opportunity to grow spiritually and earn more time to read and write my books.

"One must be humble, one must keep personal preferences and antipathies in the background, if one wishes to discover the realities of the world" (Sigmund Freud, Freemason).

Today, although I have collected hundreds of enemies during past years, and many more when my life improved drastically, I am at peace and happy with what I have achieved.

As for money, it won't help me in the after-life, and I've learned enough not to depend on it, like the majority of the brainwashed human society.

I still have things to say and share, and I will keep writing books and making sure the system brings me back the necessary amount of wealth, to keep living a life by revealing truths that can help and uplift others and the whole world altogether.

If this world wishes to make me more famous in the following years, leading me to be more important than many, that are now and shouldn't be, as they're just reinforcing the system pushed in front of society, that isn't in my plans or goals.

Being invisible has been the best thing I've learned to do. Because you can't make everyone happy, but you can always create enemies if you make significant changes in the world.

We are never completely out of the system, but we can become independent from it. And thanks to the knowledge exposed in this book, I'm now complete within myself, so I wish for you that you obtain the same.

Changes change as much as you want to change, and there're many ways to look at life, but only one thing makes the difference: Are you happy with yours?

Chapter 95: How to Deprogram Yourself.

The programming of the mind reveals itself in several common affirmations such as,...

- "Only rich people attract money";
- "Money comes from hard work";
- "Work comes before pleasure";
- "Only smart people get money";
- "Only people with college degrees are successful";
- "In order to achieve our goals, it is necessary to first have money";
- "Money belongs to evil people".

The list could continue. But those who succeed in life, follow very different affirmations. You can actually notice their beliefs when they speak, as they always contradict the masses.

Our brain acts as a filter of what is perceived in our reality, so if the previous list of beliefs filters the perception of opportunities in life, dreams and wishes, we will always perceive our existence as limited, and without any potential for change.

This is what we have been told to believe and what most people accept, and tends to be reinforced in our interactions with others, if we spend most of our time with individuals that think like us.

In order to deprogram yourself, become free from social programming, and get what you want from life, follow the following steps:

- Write everything that you wish to obtain in life on a piece of paper;

- Divide it in columns;

- Below each goal, write your beliefs about it;

- Then, write the opposite every time it is a negative belief;

- And finally, write a justification for each affirmation you wrote;

- Go to a mirror and repeat your positive beliefs only.

Follow this routine every morning, until you feel comfortable with the affirmations, as that is when the negative charge of your beliefs has been cleaned.

If you want to obtain faster results, create small cards and read the affirmations every day in your spare time, such as when waiting for the bus or subway, or in a waiting-room, starting by the ones that make you feel more uncomfortable.

You can also improve faster, if you choose goals that seem more realistic to you, such as earning a certain amount of extra money every month, instead of wishing something abstract to you, like becoming a billionaire.

The following is an example of how to apply it:

- Wish: Earn an extra $2000 every month;

- Column: Money;

- Belief: I'm not smart enough to earn more, I don't have good ideas to earn more and I don't have time to do anything else;

- Opposite Belief: I can learn, I can have profitable ideas and I can create more time;

- Justification: Last year I learned how to cook French food; 5 years before that, I sold my car; and I can wake up early on Saturday to work on my ideas;

- Self-deprogramming: Go to a mirror and repeat the previous affirmations and justifications while looking at your eyes: "I can learn, because last year I learned how to cook French food; I can have profitable ideas, because 5 years ago I was able to sell my car and make money from it; and I can create more time to work on my ideas by walking up early on Saturdays."

As a result, you will first start feeling more confident, and then you'll notice that, once in a while, you get an idea about what you can do to achieve your goals or an intuition about things you should be doing to clear the way for your ideas to come, such as selling your non-useful items in the house, donate stuff, etc.

If you repeat these affirmations with a smile, your body relaxes and it is easier to get rid of the discomfort of contradicting old beliefs.

Education, the media and culture, did a very good job in programming you with observable facts, but it is possible to find the opposite facts to deprogram you on anything, especially in regarding to beliefs about money.

If you find it difficult, technology can help you, as you can type on internet things like,...

- "How I learned";
- "How I got profitable ideas";
- "How I created time in my life".

You will realize that there are many people in the world that can do this and have done it. But you can also type,...

- "How to learn";
- "How to get an idea";
- "How to gain time".

The more you search, the more likely you are to find everything you need.

A spiritual being always finds opportunities outside his physical universe.

If you really want to change your life, you will find the opportunities. They are being shared by those who have found some of the ones you need.

Chapter 96: Delusional and Realistic Dreams.

The problem with most people is that, they are so trapped in their life and problems, which they have accumulated and learned to accept, they then try to learn from blogs and books with titles like "how to become a millionaire" or "how to get money".

Concepts like millionaire and money are abstract and part of a delusional world, so you won't be able to understand the application of the knowledge, if you keep thinking with the same paradigm that made you poor.

I had a friend that wanted to become rich but couldn't even find a job.

I saw his resume and invited him to perform a training interview with me. The result was clear, as he didn't know how to behave, and his resume didn't prove his competence in any field where he wanted to work.

I told him how to behave in a job interview and changed his resume to a much more professional description and presentation. And just a few days after, he was receiving many calls for job interviews. Less than a month later he got a job.

One year passed, and with the money accumulated from this new job, he decided to start a business. But one month after, it was bankrupt. And he couldn't understand why he failed, so I offered him many business magazines I had, with biographies of successful entrepreneurs.

From those readings, he realized that a business in real-estate was the fastest way to become rich. But, in one year, he only sold one house and didn't know what was wrong.

After a brief conversation, it was clear that he didn't have any experience in selling anything, didn't know how to communicate with others, and wasn't learning anything about his business.

Therefore, I bought him two books about the experience of famous real-estate agents.

He seemed very happy to receive those books, but in the next day, told me that he didn't agree with what he was reading, and didn't thought they would apply in his situation.

I also suggested different strategies to market his houses, but he didn't feel comfortable with the ideas and didn't follow them as well.

The truth is that he will never be a successful person, because he isn't connected to his dream, but merely the illusion of making money.

He did not even say "thank you" for my gifts and information, or invited me out for dinner, which shows that he does not know how to appreciate the opportunities that life gives him. He has a very poor soul.

Quite often, from what I observed in many people, this is their main problem. They have no respect for those who help them.

People like me show up in their life, and they either insult or ignore. And that is the real reason why they are poor: They are stupid! But it's a special kind of stupidity.

I use the word stupid here, not as related to the lack of knowledge, but the rejection of knowledge and opportunities. Because that is what being stupid really means.

You are not stupid because you don't know something. You are certainly stupid when someone offers you a book with the information you need, but you refuse to read it.

Chapter 97: How Your Attitude Can Make You Wealthy.

It is easy for me to see the difficulties others have to accumulate wealth, not just due to my life experience as a business consultant, but also because people show me very clear behavior patterns.

The alchemical steps to attract success are always the same, although manifested differently in each individual.

In order to illustrate this using more examples, I will mention two of my former students. One got rich before finishing her major, by simply focusing in what she loved to do and what she had to learn to be able to do it.

Her major was in languages and she loved to travel, so she studied Portuguese, Spanish and English, went to South America as an exchange student, offered her services online to Chinese tourists, and then, in her spare time, traveled with those individuals while making tons of money.

After one year, she went back to China because she had to finish her major, but told me that she could already afford an independent lifestyle in South America or Europe.

The other, was graduating in teaching, but didn't like it, and so, as I suggested her, she went to the United States to explore other possibilities in life, made many friends and experienced something new, like teaching children with learning disabilities, and loved it.

She then decided to apply for a Master's degree in the United States, in the field of learning disabilities, and with my recommendation letter, she was chosen in the exact University she wanted.

She's now very happy with her new life and knows exactly what she wants for the future.

These stories have me as the main character in them, but my advice, contrary to the many other cases, was not neglected, but followed until the end. So we must admit that attitude is what determines success, and not necessary the lack or not of opportunities.

If we have guidance in life, like those two students, and we trust it, like the words of a successful and popular lecturer, it's much easier.

Egocentrism and pride is what make us neglect the perspective of friends that are doing their best to help us, as it was the situation of one of my friends. But "God does not love the arrogant" (The Bee, In The Quran).

I could disclose many more stories, because I have seen the same principle being applied dozens of times, and not even necessarily due to my own knowledge being exposed.

The most impressive experience, happened to me before I quit working as a lecturer, when I decided to show a video in the classroom about business.

Only one student, among 80, approached me in the end of the class, asking to copy the video, and inviting me for lunch to ask more questions about it.

As we were eating, she wrote everything I said, about how to connect the principles of the video with her ambitions, which seemed very simple and naive, but would determine her whole future.

She was the only student in that class that never needed to search for a job, because she created her own company and is still successfully managing it.

She even employed two of her former classmates.

She changed her entire life in one day, and she wasn't even among the brightest students. So, "let us sacrifice one day to gain perhaps a whole life" (Victor Hugo, Rosicrucian Fellowship).

Chapter 98: Help Creates Bridges Towards Your Dreams.

The main problem with most people is that, once they start failing in life, they believe their situation is hopeless, and because of that attitude, they don't believe in being helped.

When you are attracting the future you wish to have, you'll first either attract people that want to help you, helpful ideas or information that helps. And in order for these situations to manifest within your spectrum of awareness, you must believe that you can be helped and develop faith in yourself.

Taking into consideration what I've seen, if I had to divide people into successful and unsuccessful with one single word, I would use faith, and with three words, I would say: Belief in help!

You must believe in help, if you want to be helped. "You feel alive to the degree that you feel you can help others" (John Travolta, Scientology).

This belief will expand your awareness, making you notice things that you couldn't see before, while gaining ideas and insights that you never had.

Whatever you see or think about when this process is occurring, it's always personal, so don't expect others to understand or even accept it.

When I decided to become a writer, I had a strong feeling from within, that I should leave my country behind and experience a new reality. I couldn't understand why, but I followed my instinct.

Years later, I realized that this instinct was related to my love for writing, as by traveling I met many amazing people that inspired me, experienced new things that made me get more ideas for my books, and gained much more time to write than I could ever imagine.

If I hadn't done it, I wouldn't have succeeded. But when I decided to leave my country, every single person tried to persuade me to stay, using strong justifications to prove they were right.

One person owned a private school and offered me a management position with a partnership in her business, in which I would gain a 50% profit in extracurricular activities developed.

She said I was crazy in refusing this opportunity for another, in which I would earn far much less and just be a teacher.

My friends also said that it was crazy to leave the country for a less profitable opportunity. And my family said it would be wiser to try to find a job in a richer country instead.

The main point is that nobody believed I could make a career as a writer, and that was the reason I had not to listen to any of them, because that was my dream. The rest was secondary to me, although they were seeing it as crucial, namely, the country, the salary and leaving them behind.

We shouldn't waste our life living someone else's project for our existence. "To be understood is to prostitute oneself" (Fernando Pessoa, Rosicrucian Fellowship).

There is only one way in life and that's forward. But it is difficult to move forward with the experiences of the past in your memory.

If you want to reprogram your mind, you must rewrite the story of your life, by starting with the positive aspects of your past.

- First, you must write about the most positive things accomplished and experienced in the past;

- Then write about the goals that you would want to achieve;

- End this exercise by reading the story to a recorder. Mix the result with your favorite music, using one that doesn't have any lyrics. You can use sound editing software for this purpose. And when the recording is finished, just put your earphones and listen before going to bed every night.

You can do the same thing for beliefs you wish to have, by repeating things like:

- "You can learn";
- "You can make more money";
- "You are smart";
- "You are beautiful", etc.

You don't have to worry about how contradictory your reality may seem, as in time many things will happen that will shift it, such as obtaining new ideas, meeting new people, getting new opportunities and having new experiences.

All these things will push you in a completely new direction.

At the end of it, you will find yourself exactly where you should be.

Some of the first changes to experience may seem dramatic, if you suddenly lose your job and friends start leaving your life, or if you start failing in certain aspects of what you usually do, or your spouse leaves you. But, from another perspective, this is the first manifestation of the alchemical transmutation before you enter a new path in your life.

Free will, means that others also have their own karma to experience, and may not be part of the reality you are creating for yourself. You must respect that!

You must remain aware that everyone you love has their own path, and such path may not include yours.

Most people try to keep what they are losing, or become depressed about what they can't maintain, but the right attitude is to accept change, and have faith in a bright new future, because you must be aware of the opportunities that any calamity brings.

"Failure is simply the opportunity to begin again, this time more intelligently" (Henry Ford, Loyal Order of Moose).

Chapter 99: How to Reprogram Emotional Responses.

Your attitude to your efforts, will determine if you can keep up with them, or suddenly start losing interest in following your life plan.

Most people can't finish a project or apply an idea, because they don't have enough willpower to move it forward. But this exercise will teach you how to gain it:

- Write about a task that you are avoiding or dislike doing;

- Then write how you could make the task more interesting and joyful;

- Finally, write about how you could control this task with activities.

As an example, if you dislike cooking, you can think about how you could cook while listening to music or audiobooks related to your favorite subjects.

As a control method, you can measure either how much you can learn from an audiobook while cooking, or how fast you can cook with music.

If you dislike reading, think about the possibility of reading in a garden with beautiful trees around you, and uplifting your mood.

As a control method, you could count how many pages you can read in 30min, and try to surpass that record every time you read a book.

Another control method for books, including audiobooks, is to underline, or write in a piece of paper, everything that you believe to be important for your life, and then create a short resume with those quotes, to remember and share with others.

It is very important, during this reprogramming, that you develop self-control. And you can do this by developing a sense of responsibility for yourself.

A good habit related to this attitude, is helping others with what you do. It's easier to get motivation to read, if you then share what you have learned with others that may need the information.

Inviting people once in a while, to have lunch with you, can also help in gaining motivation to cook well and with joy. For it is easier to help yourself when you want to help others.

My books were often inspired by conversations with others, and in which I shared my knowledge related to their questions and problems in life.

It is because I have a strong will to help other people, that I keep getting insights and ideas to write new books. And in many situations, books also emerged from inspired emails.

The same happened to me when I was DJing, organizing music events, and even when managing companies. Those companies profited with my work and started obtaining fast results, because I had a strong desire to help the group working with me.

"To fulfill a dream, you must forget it, remove your attention from it" (Fernando Pessoa, Rosicrucian).

You do this by submerging into the love you have for what you do.

This book, for example, was possible due to my strong desire to share this knowledge with others, and not because I intended to be recognized, sell thousands of copies and become popular with it, as it ended up happening.

It was what I dreamed, but not where I had put my attention when creating it, and not the reason that led me to write it.

I've also noticed that most people that have met me in person, can't learn from me, because they are focusing either in my reputation or their purpose. They end up asking the wrong questions, questions that lead nowhere.

The ones that benefited from me, were just being themselves, and honesty led them to the acknowledgement they needed to acquire.

Chapter 100: The Process of Becoming Self-Aware.

Every time you go out of the house, you'll arrive back with a changed vibration, usually affected by a stressful work or unfriendly people.

It is normal that everyone, currently in your reality, affects you with their belief in regarding to who you are or should be, so they'll be part of the challenge of changing yourself as they'll resist it.

In order to make your body resonate a new vibration all the time, you can do a visualization exercise:

- Search for images of what you wish to attract in life in the internet, and then put them altogether in a folder of your computer;

- At the end of the day, put some nice music and observe your images, one by one, as a slideshow in the screen of the computer. If you wish, you can also use software to create a video with those images and your favorite music playing in the background;

- Watch the images or video until you feel more relaxed, and in tune with your new chosen vibration of happiness and accomplishment;

- Then, close your eyes, with a straight back and the head aligned with your shoulders, and relax the shoulders, and empty your thoughts by imagining a white screen. Stay in this position for a few minutes, until you find yourself feeling at peace. The whole exercise should last about 10 minutes and must be kept as a daily routine, in order to wash your mind after washing your body.

To obtain a new future, you must leave the past behind. An exercise that you can do to train yourself, consists in closing your eyes, and visualizing those that have hurt you or those that have programmed negative beliefs in you.

Then, say to them:

— "I forgive you for... and I let you go".

When finishing it, say to yourself:

— "From this negative experience, I have learned something positive, and it was..."

End the exercise by saying to yourself:

— "I've changed and I'm now in a new path. I'm a new person".

Repeat this exercise every time you feel inner blocks regarding what you wish to obtain in life.

Here's an example of how to say it:

— "I forgive Mary for making me believe that money comes from hard work, and I let her go;

From this negative experience, I've learned something positive, and it was that people have their own beliefs, but I must be independent if I wish to have a different life;

I've changed and I'm now in a new path. I'm a new person".

Remember that we become what we believe that we should be, so resentment may stop us from realizing it.

Resentment and victimization affects your vibration, and leads you to attract challenges related to more situations that make you feel like a victim and resentful.

People that behave in a way that hurts others, aren't within the light of God, and they don't know why they do it, except for the unreasonable pleasure that they feel.

In other words, they're very sick from a mental and spiritual point of view.

You must recognize this fact in order to forgive them, even though you don't have to accept them. We must learn to forgive those that live in darkness.

The more conscious you are in regarding to how your own surroundings affects you, the more you'll be in control of your life and wishes.

As you apply the knowledge exposed in this book, you'll start seeing more about the codes that program the society around you, and that's when you realize that seeing is more important than having.

"The highest manifestation of life consists in this: that a being governs its own actions" (Thomas Aquinas, Catholic Priest and member of the Rosicrucian Fellowship).

Knowing how to love is more important than possessing love or avoiding hate. This is the meaning of the All-Seeing-Eye, the living consciousness of truth. And freedom comes with this awakening.

"In order to improve the mind, we ought less to learn, than to contemplate" (René Descartes, Rosicrucian Fellowship).

Chapter 101: Exercises of Mind-Control.

Obsessive thoughts and uncontrolled worries are manifestations of the power of the subconscious programming over the conscious ability of a human to think.

They are more predominant in environments charged with radiation, when under physical pain or emotional suffering, and when our health isn't in a good condition.

It is true that, when you do something outside of an inner reality, your condition improves. "To improve is to change; to be perfect is to change often" (Winston Churchill, Freemason and member of the Ancient Order of Druids of Oxford).

This happens because of our condition as spiritual beings — we learn with observation and actions. But there are tricks you can apply to control your thoughts:

- To begin with, choose one point in the horizon, a very faraway point, such as an object, a person, a bird or a house, and just observe it;

- You can change to different points in that distant horizon and, if you play golf, it is even better, as the reason why the Power Elite loves to play golf is because this sport allows practicing this skill. This is enough to clean the mind of worries and the results are usually faster than meditation.

The same principle applies in other ways, such as the observation of the corners of a room. But you can also play games with your mind, like trying to find objects of a certain color in the environment.

This will help you exercise control over the mind.

In regarding to using actions to change your condition, you can simply hold and release an object several times. You can also give orders to yourself and to the object, and then follow them.

Start by saying your name, and then give yourself a command like:

— "John, go pick up that cup of water!"

Then, say to the cup: — "Come to my hand!

Following this, you can say:

— "Thank you", And "now go back", While placing the cup back in the same place.

This last exercise may sound strange to you, but works because, as human beings, we operate with space, actions (or energy) and matter (observation or attention on physical world).

Children do this naturally, when playing with objects and roleplaying. That's how they exercise their brain and self-control, and that's also why the best exercises for hyperactive children, are those in which they use the body to interact with objects, like playing with clay or painting things.

From a quantum physics' point of view, the atoms move with conscience, so you attract that in which you focus. But by focusing on it, you also channel your energy to that observation, instead of allowing it to randomly manifest thoughts inside your mind.

This means that your reality is affected by the way you communicate with it, either it is in the form of an object, a project, or the people around you.

Communication increases your own awareness, and that's reality, but both depend on the level of affinity, acceptance and appreciation that you have with the things within your awareness.

Appreciation for what we have releases love in our magnetic field.

When we are forced to spend time in an environment, where we don't feel safe and comfortable, we can't appreciate it or feel any connection with it. Instead, we start losing self-control, losing focus, and having more thoughts inside of our mind, which eventually lead to depression, especially, if we don't have a way of compensating them with joyful activities.

Chapter 102: How to Control Your Thoughts.

Focusing (or communicating with observation) in objects and things outside of our mind, expands awareness (perception of reality), which will eventually allow us to understand that reality and, in doing so, learn to appreciate it and control much more.

"The eye of a master will do more work than both his hands" (Benjamin Franklin, Freemason and member of the Rosicrucian Fellowship).

Most people have difficulties in applying this principle when dealing with others, because at some point, their own fear controls their conscious mind.

They then start thinking more, about what to say, when to say it, how to say, etc. And when something fails, they spend the rest of the day thinking about it, and trying to find another way to control it.

If you want to learn how to control your social environment, instead of being controlled by it, and then become affected by the self-judgments of the mind programming, start by looking at people as individuals outside of your body. Observe their eyes and recognize their existence. When they speak, analyze their words and intentions. And ask questions when you don't understand something.

You may need to learn to touch them, as when handshaking every day, to make sure they are real to you as individuals, and not just a construct of your imagination.

These attitudes will help you feel better with yourself, because that's what you're supposed to do as a spirit on earth. "Wisdom is the daughter of experience" (Leonardo Da Vinci, Rosicrucian Fellowship).

It is also due to this spiritual need of interacting with the physical world, that people feel good when they work, especially in things they can create or when using the body.

The more you suffer from depression and uncontrolled thoughts, the more you need to interact with the physical world to heal.

The opposite is also true, as if you lack good communication with reality, it's because you spend too much time inside your brain, thinking. But you're not your brain, so unless you observe the thoughts from outside, you get easily trapped.

The best way to analyze a thought, and make it disappear, when it comes to you, is to write it down.

I have many thoughts because I write books, but I don't think all the time, because I control the thoughts. And you too, can control your own thoughts, by analyzing their purpose and how you can apply them.

As an example, I only think when I have to, as when I write, or when I can, such as when I'm not doing anything. But when I'm not writing or relaxing, I focus on the physical environment.

This is how you improve communication with your reality, control thoughts and feel happier, while becoming more efficient as well.

As you're made of atoms and molecules, when improving the interaction with your environment, you're actually improving your level of interaction with the energy world in which you are included.

This explains why we feel so happy when successful, as it makes us feel that we can control our energy in this world of energies. It makes us feel like we're evolving as a spirit.

As beings of light, the only thing that truly matters is this light, "God's first creature, which was light" (Sir Francis Bacon, Rosicrucian Fellowship).

The brain works with emotions, so we tend to think and analyze according to what we feel. And that's how we get trapped into believing that something makes sense, just because we feel that it is familiar to us. We then end up having inner conversations because we're not looking at things as they really are.

Chapter 103: How to Overcome Your Painful Memories.

You can't change the past and you shouldn't waste energy regretting it or feeling pity for yourself.

If memories emerge in your mind, when doing the exercises explained in this book, or when meditating, it is because they are still very important for you. And they are usually the first thing emerging from your awareness of your emotional suffering.

The purpose of awareness and conscious meditation, is to access negative memories holding you back, and that's why true knowledge can help in remembering them.

If you can remember the past, it means that the experience isn't as powerful to control you subconsciously as it was before. In other words, you gained more control over your own life.

If there's a benefit in meditating, it would be this one, which means relaxing enough to realize things that consciously you wouldn't.

Knowing these things increases your awareness about yourself. But what's truly important is what you do with such awareness. You shouldn't be stuck in the past, but instead use it to improve your future.

"When we go to our sanctuary, we must go as the lover who hastens to his beloved – our spirit must fly ahead of our slow/moving body in eager anticipation of the delights in store for us, and we must forget all else in the thoughts of adoration which fill us on the way.

This is literally true: the feeling required for success resembles nothing in the world so much as that which draws the lover to his beloved; it is even more ardent and intense" (Max Heindel, Rosicrucian Fellowship).

Quite often, the pain related to past experiences, is holding you back from finding your life purpose, and conditioning your thoughts, over yourself and your experiences, and even how you make decisions.

A decision is a conscious act and random thoughts are subconscious manifestations. So when you have to make a conscious decision, as when realizing what makes you happy, but you have thoughts making you think about something else or doubting it, it is not that the thoughts that matter but their purpose.

In this situation, usually the purpose is to make you doubt yourself and your potential, with ideas like "I can't do it", "I can fail", etc.

These thoughts can emerge from another perspective as well, such as: "What would a successful person do?"

One way or another, they're related to a feeling — disbelief in yourself, and this feeling is related to a strong emotional and negative experience in your past.

The reason why you get trapped in thoughts, if you focus on them, is that the thought is subconscious and therefore it consumes your energy.

Analysis is a conscious act, so the ability to analyze something is the ability to control thoughts. Your purpose must then be to know which thoughts are controlling you and why, where do they come from, and who or what made them stay there as "emotional buttons" controlling your mind.

You can write your negative self-beliefs and then ask yourself:

- Who made me believe this?

- What experience made me believe this?

You can close your eyes, focus on the belief, and ask the questions until you get the answers.

Instead of singing a mantra, like "Om", repeat "who made me believe this?", several times, and until your subconscious answers the question with images and mind movies related to the past.

Once you know it and re-experience it as an outsider, an observer, it won't have more power over you.

The tears that may come out of this exercise, are emotional charges releasing from your body — accumulated pain vanishing away.

When this is done, you don't need to stay in that past anymore. You can forgive yourself.

The best way to heal, consists in using that awareness about past events to know what you're doing wrong in the present and then learn to be happier.

Chapter 104: The Illusion of a Timeline.

Past, Present and Future are illusions. They only exist in our mind.

Researches in quantum physics tell us that time is a construct of our brain. Although our body gets older, our spirit only experiences present time.

The question is: Why can we remember the past but not predict the future?

The answer is related to our purpose as a spiritual being. If we knew the future, we could easily avoid responsibility and delay our spiritual development.

Knowing the past allows learning with our mistakes and the mistakes of others. And so, knowing the past allows developing responsibility in the present, and with this responsibility in hands, we consciously create our future.

When we are accepting full responsibility for what we do, we start developing premonitions, insights and ideas, about what we should be doing, as if the future was manifesting to us in the same proportion of our accepted responsibility.

According to the same principle, the more you work towards achieving what you want, the more good ideas you get about how to achieve it faster.

Our visions and ideas are proportional to our accumulated responsibility.

The world is made of atoms, thoughts are made of atoms, and the future is made of atoms as well. So when you control these atoms with physical actions, and focus in the future atoms with your intentions — your vision of the future you want —, you then attract situations that reposition you, towards obtaining the power of getting it.

What for most people represents isolation, challenges and changes, is actually, from this perspective, a transmutation of the physical body to an environment where the conscious mind can more easily create a new future, the future we have desired before.

There's no accident, misfortune, disaster, coincidence or luck in life, and we can only lose that and those which we are neglecting.

You lose things because you didn't work hard enough to get them, and because you didn't believe enough in yourself; and you lose people from your life because you were too selfish to realize their needs and life purpose.

I keep finding lots of information about cancer and arthritis, marketing and money, as well as simple descriptions about the law of attraction, and I know exactly why, as it is my responsibility to act towards that knowledge, by providing it to the ones who need it.

I don't want my friends to fail in life, and I don't want my family members to die, so I keep attracting the knowledge that they need, and I take responsibility for it, by sending this information to them, and sharing it whenever I have the chance to talk to them.

This is being responsible for the ones around you, and they'll love you and respect you for your efforts in helping them, even if they can't help themselves and have no hope in life.

When you're aware of this and act accordingly, you gain control over your life. And with this positive control — which shouldn't be confused with manipulation — you get a very deep and amazing feeling of happiness, accomplishment and fulfillment.

Chapter 105: Why Some People Reject Help?

If those in need don't appreciate your help and withdraw from your life, it is because they have decided to die. When trying to help them, it is as if you were proving them wrong.

Alcoholics, drug addicts and other mentally ill individuals that reject help, are examples of people that are slowly committing suicide and intentionally.

They want you to feel guilty and negative about it, to gain pleasure from your worries. Such feeling of responsibility for their situation makes them feel alive, in some distorted way.

These individuals are the zombies and the vampires of our world, and unfortunately they are a majority.

Most people live in an extremely unconscious level of existence, and they are dangerous to your integrity and threatening to your life.

This is why sometimes you need to metaphorically slap others to make them aware of the pain they cause you, shout to impose respect and, basically, tell people what to do with their life, how to do it and why, because they just don't know anymore, and can't even realize the need to know it by themselves.

"The manifestation of neurosis or insanity is completely undirected action or inaction" (Ron Hubbard, Scientology).

This situation shows itself more necessary towards the psychopaths that control our world, and those that unconsciously and blindly support their laws, while wearing uniforms and occupying positions that should stand for peace and security.

That is why riots, manifestations and violent revolutions are inevitable, if we ever wish to maintain our freedom as human beings. "Revolutions are not born of chance but of necessity" (Victor Hugo, Rosicrucian Fellowship).

As a human race, we won't evolve, if we don't protect and support the innocent and the most enlightened souls. And as spiritual beings, we won't evolve, if we believe that what we see doesn't affect our awareness of who we are.

Keeping silent when you witness injustice is to act against your own spirituality, because nothing exists apart of your inner world.

"Silence is the virtue of fools" (Sir Francis Bacon, Rosicrucian Fellowship).

Just as you attract opportunities that lead to your dreams, you also attract experiences that test your potential to achieve them. And it's worth mentioning that, those spreading the idea that you should be positive all the time and not get angry with what you experience, are denying you the opportunity to learn to be responsible for your outcomes.

If you attract a situation that makes you angry, it means you're supposed to be angry, otherwise you'll be denying yourself the chance to impose your will, or justice, when it's being threatened, violated and disrespected.

"God did this in order to test everything within you, and in order to prove what is in your heart. God knows your innermost thoughts very well" (The Our, In The Quran).

Imagine you are inside an airplane and a terrorist threatens everyone with a weapon. Do you really think he can shoot dozens of passengers at the same time?

Believing that you can't do anything for others is what gets everyone killed in every single massacre in human history. And those that have died in the past in such situations, may have to face them again in a future reincarnation, if they can't learn the lesson.

In other words, Hitler killed the Jews as much as the Jews killed themselves, by not creating riots and violent opposition against Hitler.

As a human race, we won't evolve until we start accepting these facts, instead of pointing fingers at one another, and blaming those that we have allowed to gain power and maintain it.

The responsibility to act can be manifested as the responsibility to oppose someone or something.

Chapter 106: Those Who Choose to Live in Bubbles of Illusion.

Individuals that believe in the idea of being happy all the time, while denying themselves the chance to interfere and become angry, when a situation demands it, can't attract wealth into their life, because they are violating the same laws that they wish to fulfill. But "do you think that most of them hear or understand? They are just like cattle — no, they are further from the path" (The Differentiator, In The Quran).

If you ever wondered why kind people can't attract wealth, now you know that it's not because they're not evil, but because they fear having to oppose evil. And what you can't oppose, becomes part of you, suppressed within your subconscious.

"Unexpressed emotions will never die. They are buried alive and will come forth later in uglier ways" (Sigmund Freud, Freemason).

When you witness injustice and don't do anything about it, you prove yourself unworthy of what you want, and that's why millions of people read tons of books about the law of attraction and can't get anything decently done in their life.

As hard as it is to say it or admit it, you are responsible for your future, and you create it with what you do in the present. But this principle doesn't apply only to the positive side of life, as the negative experiences exist to show you the path to the light.

Satan works with the permission of God, and both manifest within the same living consciousness. They are both operating inside our matrix of reality.

Through different concepts and applications, this is the foundation of the Taoist and the Gnostic Philosophies. "If you correct your mind, the rest of your life will fall into place" (Lao Tzu, Founder of Taoism).

If you don't think that you have any responsibility in helping others around you, and sharing what you know with the world, then you also don't deserve the right to be helped when you need the most, and when you want to find what you need to know. Just like a father that doesn't care about loving his son, doesn't deserve to be loved back later in life, when alone and in need of love.

The reason why some people seem to know more than others, and get more opportunities and less problems than the rest, is because they're so focused in doing the best they can for the world, that they always attract the best to themselves from that same world. We must give in order to receive.

The paradox of existence is that, while you have free will to choose what you do, including the refusal to support those needing you, the ones who need your help and deserve it, will always get it in another way and from someone else. "All is forseen, yet man is endowed with free will" (Avot 3:15, In Akiba Mishna).

I never received help or respect from my parents, but I met dozens of people during my entire life that helped me, strengthen me and taught me the mysteries of life, as if I was their own son.

God guided me to the Gnostic mysteries, despite the poor and violent environment where I was growing up, because I deserved them. And with this knowledge, I made my life become the most unpredictable story anyone could have ever imagine, while transforming myself into someone unreal and impossible to exist to the limited minds of most humans.

You can even be rejected by the whole world but, if God loves you, you own the world. So "seek refuge in God: He is your protector — an excellent protector and an excellent helper (The Quran 22:71).

What is taken from you, God always gives back in another way.

Chapter 107: Where Are Our Prophets?

The idea that prophets don't get angry, when witnessing injustice and facing individuals of evil intentions, is one of the biggest lies in which people tend to believe about spirituality, as it is to believe that Jesus is the individual that mainstream christians and christian movies tend to portray.

When aware of malice, Jesus confronted others with the words:

— "Why do you put me to the test, you hypocrites?" (Matthew 22:18, In The Bible).

"No one can serve two Masters, for either he will hate one and love the other, or he will be devoted to one and despise the other (Matthew 6:24), but "evil people and impostors will go on from bad to worse, deceiving and being deceived (Timothy 3:13).

Jesus also said:

— "Be doers of the word, and not hearers only, deceiving yourselves, because if anyone is a hearer of the word and not a doer, he is like a man who looks intently at his natural face in a mirror, for he looks at himself and goes away and at once forget what he was like" (James 1:22-24). But the "wrath of God is revealed from heaven against all ungodliness and unrighteousness of men, who by their unrighteousness suppress the truth" (Romans 1:18).

In these Biblical words, Jesus warns us about the danger of losing our awareness and the benefits of our spirituality, when we refuse to act against injustice.

If we contribute to the suppression of truth in the form of justice, respect and love, we too suffer the wrath of God, which is manifested in the withdrawing of his positive energies from us, as well as in the attraction of difficulties and sufferings, and which come with the purpose of teaching us a lesson related to our past behavior.

As an example, those who refuse to help the ones in need, may start facing problems which nobody around them can help solve. And these problems will prevail until they feel remorse for their actions, or start helping others.

In other situations, it may seem that a person has acquired some kind of incurable disease but the source is the same.

Kind people get sick because they're too afraid to get angry when they should demand justice. Anger can only become armful when suppressed and maintained with thoughts associated with resentment and revenge.

They emerge from a subconscious need to do justice when we consciously refuse to do it. So, in fact, resentment and revengeful thoughts, are evil manifestations of spiritual weaknesses and the inability to protect the truth.

Those who succumb to such negative emotions, submerge into darkness, and may become as evil as the ones that once hurt them, although suicidal thoughts can also arise from the same outcome.

The right attitude consists in learning from the experience and taking actions towards solving it, which sometimes means exposing the truth and the liar, with the risks involved in doing it.

Other times means turning away from the situation, although this has been misinterpreted by some Christian societies as "offering the other cheek".

Chapter 108: The Challenges of Faith.

Even though most people are afraid to lose their job, it's very likely that the application of the law of attraction may bring a situation of disrespect at work, in which you're supposed to act in defense of justice and risk losing it.

Once a coworker asked me for help about salaries which my former boss was refusing to pay him. As he was an immigrant, the union refused to help him, and due to the fear of losing their own job, nobody else wanted to support him in court.

I helped him and immediately lost my job, but this coworker, in fear of not getting any money, decided to wait for an agreement with the boss, and which never happened.

As for me, God guided me into reading my working contract, and I found a mistake in it, allowing me to go to court and demand a full year of salaries with the help of the government.

Soon after my threat was official, the company asked their lawyer to talk to me, but although he was trying to trick me, God guided me again, and I ended up being very rude to that man while demanding half of that money immediately and on the table.

They quickly run to the nearest ATM machine and came back with the cash. So I dropped the charges. But what they didn't know is that, at that time in my life, I actually couldn't afford to pay a lawyer or go to court, because I had a plane to catch two days later to another country, where I had found a better job.

Surely, this isn't always as easy as it seems. I have been physically threatened many times, physically assaulted as well, and nearly murdered by poisoning for exposing the truth, but I do believe that I'm still alive because God protects those who protect the truth.

"God makes things easy for those who are mindful of Him" (Divorce, In The Quran).

Only fear can cause death, and I rather face death than fear. However, "courage is not the absence of fear, but rather the assessment that something else is more important than fear" (Franklin D. Roosevelt, Freemason and member of the Loyal Order of Moose).

Although I've grown with the idea, as most people, that heroes have special powers and strength, like superman, I later realized that the true heroes of our world are individuals like Julian Assange, Edward Snowden, Ted Gunderson and Alex Jones, who despite not having any superpower but facing the risk of being murdered at the hands of the most powerful villains in the planet, won't stop exposing the truth, even when facing ridicule by those that they are protecting the most — the human race.

Jesus may have died for the truth, but we haven't learned it yet, and this may lead us to our self-annihilation as a race on this planet.

"Every judgement of conscience, be it right or wrong, be it about things evil in themselves or morally indifferent, is obligatory, in such wise that he who acts against his conscience always sins" (Thomas Aquinas, Catholic Priest and member of the Rosicrucian Fellowship).

Chapter 109: The Truth Will Set You Free.

Awareness is you — your recognition of what exists in your conscious and subconscious mind.

When you learn more about yourself, about things that you didn't know about you, memories from the past come to present time, because they are related to the new insight.

True knowledge sets you free, because it increases awareness.

As an example, when realizing that you have a bad relationship with the world, there's a memory about the reason, an experience making you unaware of your behavior, that emerged from the subconscious, and that's why you can recall this memory.

As the conscious and the subconscious are related, and part of who you are, you can access both through one of them.

Meditation brings the subconscious to the conscious level, while knowledge about yourself increases conscience about what you didn't know before, and that's the subconscious material.

Although for most people meditation and spiritual readings seem like something outside of their reality, and even mystical, they are merely exercises to empower you as a spiritual being, and give you the opportunity to be fully responsible for your life.

From a scientific point of view, when you know who you are and who you aren't, you develop awareness of your past, realizing both what influenced you negatively and positively. When this happens, you become more conscious of what you should be doing in your life, which means that you become more aware of your responsibilities as a spiritual individual.

As you take actions based on this awareness, you will start developing a better relationship with your environment.

This positive interaction with your work, people around you, and decisions you have to make, increases your happiness and your potential level of success.

Within this increase of control over the present time, you start postulating more possibilities about the future, because as you have more trust in your potential, you are also less afraid of what you want in life.

These ideas and postulates are as important as your memories. Because, as humans, we have memories to develop self-awareness, and we dream to develop control over the environment around us.

When you focus in a dream, you are communicating with the future, which allows developing intuition and insights about that future, namely, by avoiding mistakes. It is you communicating with the potential future and literally being in the future.

The difficulty in doing this, comes from the relationship that your energy is keeping with the past.

The more pain you have inside of yourself, the less awareness you have in present time; and the less awareness you have, the less you can dream about the future. It is as if your spirit was in another dimension while, your body is only in this one.

If you are separated from your body, you can't truly control it. People stuck in the past do more mistakes, have more accidents and hurt others more as well. But those living in the future, are more efficient, organized, faster and kinder, because they're controlling their life towards an ideal.

"The future has many names: For the weak, it means the unattainable. For the fearful, it means the unknown. For the courageous, it means opportunity" (Victor Hugo, Rosicrucian Fellowship).

Chapter 110: The True Cause of Death.

In nature, nothing is stable. Nobody is stuck in present time.

People that perform routines, as if they were in the present, are actually stuck and trapped by fears and memories. And because they don't take actions towards creating a better future, life controls them randomly.

That is why most people get easily depressed.

- They think they are their job and their friends, so when losing these elements, they lose their own self-belief.

- They also think they are what others think, so when others disrespect them, ridicule them or reject them, they lose confidence.

In other words, as time goes by, the ones that think they are in the present, are actually becoming stuck in a past that was once present.

They then keep talking about the jobs they lost, the friends they lost, the problems that certain individuals created in their life, the people that died, etc.

When they're not within their conscious present, working towards a brighter future, their energy is stuck in that past and stealing energy from their body. As the body gets weaker, these individuals develop more diseases, and eventually die.

While most people think that death is inevitable, and diseases like cancer are normal, diseases are in fact connected to the immune system, and how oxygen and detoxification are processed within our blood, which is influenced by our control of the physical body.

This control of the physical body, is related to the control over physical reality as well. We have more energy to fightback diseases when we have more control over our life.

Within this paradigm, the best cure in the world consists in believing in a dream, because, while projecting our spirit into the future, the energy holding us back in the past, and accumulating by association the atoms of the present, is redirected to the extension of life, while redirecting those atoms into the future.

Philosophically speaking, the more you trust in a bright future, the less likely you are to die.

"Prayer, true scientific prayer, is one of the most powerful and efficacious methods of finding favor before the face of our Father, and receiving the immersion in spiritual light which alchemically transforms" (Max Heindel, Rosicrucian Fellowship).

Awareness is a source of energy. Therefore, the only natural death is the death of the physical body by old age, in which dying peacefully during sleep, after a long and fulfilling life, is the best example.

As a spirit, we are immortal, so awareness increases our potential to also experience a better immortality. And those who are more aware, are able to select a new body that will then help them continue their work in a new manifestation.

Those who aren't, become trapped in the afterlife, with regrets, anxieties and attachments.

Moreover, our physical body is related to the physical world, so as our world evolves into a less dense materialization of matter, our physical bodies can live longer. And what this means is that, if human beings increase their responsibility, awareness and sense of love, as a community of one single brotherhood, our planet uplifts faster, and the next generations will live longer.

Those next generations are us, re-experiencing our joys and ambitions.

Love is immortal and eternal, and so can we become — immortal and eternal.

Chapter 111: Important Quotes to Remember.

This chapter resumes the most important quotes from this book that you must remember.

Notice that there is a greater abundance of quotes about society, determinism and consciousness, and only two quotes about money and success. Because, if you truly want to be rich and successful, money and success should be the least important things in your mind.

The greatest barriers that you will face in the path to your goals, will come from the masses — society. Without determinism and consciousness, you won't be able to overcome them.

Money and success are merely the resulting outcomes from your efforts, productivity and wise application of everything that you have learned in this book.

Everyone wants to be rich and successful, but without the right mindset, knowledge and determination, they will never reach such goals.

It is persistence that leads you there, and it starts with action — the action of reading and implementing what you have learned from me.

It is my pleasure to see you succeed with these great secrets that took me a lifetime to find and were revealed to me specifically.

14 Quotes About Society

1

"The majority are unable to see beneath the surface of the physical body and thus to perceive the true state of the thoughts and feelings of others."

—Max Heindel, Rosicrucianism

2

"It is a predisposition of human nature to consider an unpleasant idea untrue, and then it is easy to find arguments against it."

—Sigmund Freud, Freemasonry

3

"Men are not prisoners of fate, but only prisoners of their own minds."

—Franklin D. Roosevelt, Freemasonry and Loyal Order of Moose

4

"An individual must rise above an avid craving for agreement from a humanoid group to get anything decent done."

—Ron Hubbard, Scientology

5

"Ordinary morality is only for ordinary people."

—Aleister Crowley, Ordo Templi Orientis and United Order of the Golden Cross

6

"Most people do not really want freedom, because freedom involves responsibility, and most people are frightened by responsibility."

—Sigmund Freud, Freemasonry

7

"You can't build a reputation on what you are going to do."

—Henry Ford, Freemasonry and Loyal Order of Moose

8

"As human beings we have two states of consciousness: one is this world, and the other is the world beyond."

—Brihadaranyaka Upanishad

9

"If you're explaining, you're losing."

—Ronald E. Reagan, Knights of Malta

10

"When a man assumes a public trust he should consider himself a public property"

—Thomas Jefferson, Rosicrucianism

11

"A thing which is always subject to the direction of another is somewhat of a dead thing."

—Thomas Aquinas, Catholicism and Rosicrucianism

12

"To be understood is to prostitute oneself."

—Fernando Pessoa, Rosicrucianism

13

"The future has many names: For the weak, it means the unattainable. For the fearful, it means the unknown. For the courageous, it means opportunity."

—Victor Hugo, Rosicrucianism

14

"If we all worked on the assumption that what is accepted as true is really true, there would be little hope of advance."

—Orville Wright, Freemasonry

14 Quotes About Determinism

1

"Will is the dynamic soul-force."

—Albert Pike, Freemasonry and Ku Klux Klan

2

"Except our own thoughts, there is nothing absolutely in our power."

—René Descartes, Rosicrucianism

3

"Full responsibility is not fault; it is recognition of being cause."

—Ron Hubbard, Scientology

4

"Self-confidence is itself self-determinism. It is one's belief in one's ability to determine his own causes."

—L. Ron Hubbard, Scientology

5

"Courage could be summed up in: one, being willing to cause something, and two, going ahead to achieve the effect one has postulated against any and all odds."

—Ron Hubbard, Scientology

6

"I can fight only for something that I love, love only what I respect, and respect only what I at least know."

—Adolf Hitler, Thule Society, Skulls & Bones and Knights of Malta

7

"Never forget that the most powerful force on earth is love."

—Nelson A. Rockefeller, Knights of Pythias

6

"Where the heart runs, the mind chases; where God goes, the heart follows."

—Allama Prabhu, Lingaytism

7

"Nothing can stop the man with the right mental attitude from achieving his goal."

—Thomas Jefferson, Rosicrucianism

8

"To one who has faith, no explanation is necessary, and to one without faith, no explanation is possible."

—Thomas Aquinas, Catholicism and Rosicrucianism

9

"Let us sacrifice one day to gain perhaps a whole life."

—Victor Hugo, Rosicrucianism

10

"You feel alive to the degree that you feel you can help others"

—John Travolta, Scientology

11

"Failure is simply the opportunity to begin again, this time more intelligently."

—Henry Ford, Freemasonry and Loyal Order of Moose

12

"To improve is to change; to be perfect is to change often."

—Winston Churchill, Freemasonry and Ancient Order of Druids of Oxford

13

"Courage is not the absence of fear, but rather the assessment that something else is more important than fear."

—Franklin D. Roosevelt, Freemasonry and Loyal Order of Moose

14

"No matter how hard the past, you can always begin again"

—Siddhārtha Gautama, Buddhism

12 Quotes About Consciousness

1

"Nothing exists except through human consciousness."

—George Orwell, Freemasonry

2

"One man is equivalent to all creation; one man is a world in miniature."

—Albert Pike, Freemasonry and Ku Klux Klan

3

"Every man must find out for himself in what particular fashion he can be saved."

—Sigmund Freud, Freemasonry

4

"We must pass through the darkness to reach the light."

—Albert Pike, Freemasonry and Ku Klux Klan

5

"Those that have seen the boundary between the real and unreal, have acquired all knowledge."

—Bhagavad Gita

6

"All our knowledge is the offspring of our perceptions."

—Leonardo Da Vinci, Rosicrucianism

7

"The degree of simplicity is proportional to the degree of confront; knowledge is observation and is given to those who would look"

—Ron Hubbard, Scientology

8

"Those that combine action with meditation, cross the sea of death to the land of immortality."

—Upanishads

9

"We cannot command Nature except by obeying her."

—Sir Francis Bacon, Rosicrucianism

10

"The gnostic light takes us as students, and by persisting in our efforts, we suddenly get an answer to that quest."

—Jan Van Rijckenborgh, Rosicrucianism

11

"When someone searching for a new life connects in a way that is progressively more pure towards his most desirable goal, reaches a moment in which a storm begins, stays and doesn't vanish. The radiations of the new magnetic field won't abandon him. They are continually around him, inside him and assume the direction of his life. Once here, we must deal with two magnetic fields."

—Jan Van Rijckenborgh, Rosicrucianism

12

"To perceive the Divine Light which alone can illuminate our spiritual darkness, and to hear the voice of the silence which alone can guide us, we must cultivate our spiritual eyes and ears."

—Max Heindel, Rosicrucianism

10 Quotes About God

1

"Remember the Lord your God, for it is He that gives the power to make wealth."

—Deuteronomy, The Bible

2

"God truly loves those who fight in solid lines for His cause, like a well-compacted wall."

—Solid Lines, The Quran

3

"God will be enough for those who put their trust in Him."

—Divorce, The Q'uran

4

"God leaves whoever He will to stray and guides whoever He will. Do not waste your soul away with regret for them: God knows exactly what they do."

—The Creator, The Q'uran

5

"God's promise is true, so do not let the present life deceive you."

—The Creator, The Q'uran

6

"God does not love the arrogant."

—The Bee, The Quran

7

"Seek refuge in God: He is your protector - an excellent protector and an excellent helper"

—The Q'uran

8

"God makes things easy for those who are mindful of Him."

—Divorce, The Q'uran

9

"God desires, man dreams, and work is done."

—Fernando Pessoa, Rosicrucianism

10

"Prayer, true scientific prayer, is one of the most powerful and efficacious methods of finding favor before the face of our Father, and receiving the immersion in spiritual light which alchemically transforms."

—Max Heindel, Rosicrucianism

7 Quotes About Value

1

"You don't get paid for the hour; you get paid for the value you bring to the hour"

—Jim Rohn, Freemasonry

2

"What we have done for others and the world remains and is immortal."

—Albert Pike, Freemasonry and Ku Klux Klan

3

"If a person thinks he can be happy without making those around him happy, he's crazy."

—Ron Hubbard, Scientology

4

"Do not neglect your gift. Use it and you will prosper"

—Timothy, The Bible

5

"A wise man will make more opportunities than he finds."

—Francis Bacon, Freemasonry and Rosicrucianism

6

"Your greatest ability is getting an idea."

—Ron Hubbard, Scientology

7

"There's only one purpose for which a man should acquire wealth beyond the needs of his family: to help others."

—Valluvar, Hinduism

7 Quotes About Dreams and Ideas

1

"Everything in creation is governed by the law of love."

—Antonio Terrer Hernández, Rosicrucianism

2

"All visible things arise from that which is invisible."

—Bhagavad Gita

3

"Were we as we should be, We wouldn't need any illusions."

—Fernando Pessoa, Rosicrucianism

4

"Under no circumstances has force ever worked! An idea any day of the week can lick the pants off of force."

—Ron Hubbard, Scientology

5

"This dream, like the winged messenger, seems to be divinely inspired and hints at the opportunity that is about to present itself."

—Soror E.A.S., Rosicrucianism

6

"A seed is useless and impotent unless it is put in its appropriate matrix"

—Christian Rosenkreuz, Rosicrucianism

7

"When we go to our sanctuary we must go as the lover who hastens to his beloved – our spirit must fly ahead of our slow/moving body in eager anticipation of the delights in store for us, and we must forget all else in the thoughts of adoration which fill us on the way. This is literally true: the feeling required for success resembles nothing in the world so much as that which draws the lover to his beloved; it is even more ardent and intense"

—Max Heindel, Rosicrucianism

6 Quotes About Wisdom

1

"If you correct your mind, the rest of your life will fall into place."

—Lao Tzu, Taoism

2

"All is forseen, yet man is endowed with free will"

—Avot, Akiba Mishna

3

"The only true wisdom is in knowing you know nothing."

—Socrates, Pythagorean Brotherhood

4

"We can't have full knowledge all at once. We must start by believing; then afterwards we may be led on to master the evidence for ourselves."

—Thomas Aquinas, Catholicism and Rosicrucianism

5

"The eye of a master will do more work than both his hands."

—Benjamin Franklin, Freemasonry and Rosicrucianism

6

"Wisdom is the daughter of experience."

—Leonardo Da Vinci, Rosicrucianism

4 Quotes About Freedom

1

"Freedom is the possibility of isolation. You are free if you can withdraw from people, not having to seek them out for the sake of money, company, love, glory or curiosity, none of which can thrive in silence and solitude."

—Fernando Pessoa, Rosicrucianism

2

"Blessed are those who entrust their lives to no one."

—Fernando Pessoa, Rosicrucianism

3

"If you can't live alone, you've born a slave."

—Fernando Pessoa, Rosicrucianism

4

"The liberty of the individual is no gift of civilization. It was greatest before there was any civilization."

—Sigmund Freud, Freemasonry

2 Quotes About Success

1

"Success isn't immediate. Mistakes are needed to learn about what is useful or not. This is how purification occurs."

—Jan Van Rijckenborgh, Rosicrucianism

2

"The simplicity of observation is functional and will take Men from the bottom to the top."

—Ron Hubbard, Scientology

2 Quotes About Money

1

"Money is simply a symbol that people are confident can be converted into goods."

—Ron Hubbard, Scientology

2

"Virtue has never been as respectable as money."

—Mark Twain, Freemasonry

Chapter 112: Bibliography.

Baker CJ. 1995. The development _of a theoretical model for the windthrow of plants. Journal of Theoretical Biology 175, 355-72.

Gardiner BA. 1989. Mechanical characteristics of Sitka Spruce. Forestry Commission Occasional Paper No. 24.

Gardiner BA. 1995. The interaction of wind and tree movement in forest canopies. In: Coutts M, Grace J, eds. Wind and trees. Cambridge University PTess, 41-59.

Guitard DGE, Castera P. 1995. Experimental analysis and mechanical modelling of wind induced tree sways. In: Coutts

M, Grace J, eds. Wind and trees. Cambridge University Press, 182-94.

Milne R. 1991. Dynamics of swaying Picea sitchenis. Tree Physiology 9, 383-99.

Peltola H. 1995. Studies on the mechanism of wind induced damage of Scots pine. PhD thesis, University of

Joenssu, Finland.

Roodbaraky HJ, Baker CJ, Dawson AR, Wright CJ. 1994.

Experimental observations of urban trees in high winds. Journal of Wind Engineering and Industrial

Aerodynamics 52, 171-84.

Wood CJ. 1995. Understanding wind forces on trees. In: Coutts

M, Grace J, eds. Wind and trees. Cambridge University Press, 133-64.

Levy, S, 2011. In The Plex: How Google Thinks, Works, and Shapes Our Lives. Simon & Schuster.

Abrams, H. Leon. Vegetarianism: An Anthropological/Nutritional Evaluation, Jnl of Applied Nutrition,

32:2, 1980.

The Preference for Animal Protein and Fat: A Cross-Cultural Survey, Food and Evolution, Marvin Harris

and Eric Ross, eds., Temple University Press, 1987.

Diorio, L.P., et al The Separate Effects of Protein and Calorie Malnutrition of the Development and

Growth of Rat Bone and Teeth, Jnl of Nutrition 103:856-865, 1973.

Fallon, Sally. Nasty, Brutish, and Short? The Ecologist, Jan/Feb 1999.

Menaker & Navia Jnl of Dental Research, 52:680-687, 1973.

Navia, J. Nutrition, Diet, and Oral Health, Food and Nutrition News, 50:1-4, 1979.

Price, W. Nutrition and Physical Degeneration, Keats Publishing, 1943.

Spencer & Kramer Factors Contributing to Osteoporosis, Jnl of Nutr, 116:316-319, 1986.

Further Studies of the Effect of a High Protein Diet as Meat on Calcium Metabolism, Amer Jnl Clin Nutr,

June 924-929, 1983.

E. Williams and S. Heckman, "The local diurnal variation of cloud electrification and the global diurnal

variation of negative charge on the Earth," Journal of Geophysical Research, vol. 98, no. 3, pp. 5221–5234, 1993.

S. Anisimov, E. Mareev, and S. Bakastov, "On the generation and evolution of aeroelectric structures in the surface layer," Journal of Geophysical Research D, vol. 104, no. 12, pp. 14359–14367, 1999.

J. L. Oschman, "Perspective: assume a spherical cow: the role of free or mobile electrons in bodywork, energetic and movement therapies," Journal of Bodywork and Movement Therapies, vol. 12, no. 1, pp. 40–57, 2008. J. L. Oschman, "Charge transfer in the living matrix," Journal of Bodywork and Movement Therapies, vol.

13, no. 3, pp. 215–228, 2009.

D. Holiday, R. Resnick, and J. Walker, Fundamentals of Physics, Fourth Edition, John Wiley & Sons, New

York, NY, USA, 1993.

31

W. Rossi, The Sex Life of the Foot and Shoe, vol. 61, Wordsworth Editions, Hertfordshire, UK, 1989.

R. Stein, Is Modern Life Ravaging Our Immune Systems? Washington Post, 2008.

A. Just, Return to Nature: The True Natural Method of Healing and Living and The True Salvation of the

Soul, B. Lust, New York, NY, USA, 1903.

G. White, The Finer Forces of Nature in Diagnosis and Therapy, Phillips Printing Company, Los Angeles,

Calif, USA, 1929.

C. Ober, "Grounding the human body to neutralize bioelectrical stress from static electricity and EMFs,"

ESD Journal, January 2000.

K. Sokal and P. Sokal, "Earthing the human body influences physiologic processes," Journal of Alternative and Complementary Medicine, vol. 17, no. 4, pp. 301–308, 2011.

C. Ober, S. T. Sinatra, and M. Zucker, Earthing: The Most Important Health Discovery Ever? Basic Health Publications, Laguna Beach, Calif, USA, 2010.

M. Ghaly and D. Teplitz, "The biologic effects of grounding the human body during sleep as measured by cortisol levels and subjective reporting of sleep, pain, and stress," Journal of Alternative and Complementary Medicine, vol. 10, no. 5, pp. 767–776, 2004.

"NIH State-of-the-Science Conference on Manifestations and Management of Chronic Insomnia in Adults", June 13-15, 2005.

R. Applewhite, "The effectiveness of a conductive patch and a conductive bed pad in reducing induced human body voltage via the application of earth ground," European Biology and Bioelectromagnetics, vol. 1, pp. 23–40, 2005.

R. Feynman, R. Leighton, and M. Sands, The Feynman Lectures on Physics, vol. II, Addison-Wesley, Boston, Mass, USA, 1963.

K. S. Jamieson, H. M. ApSimon, S. S. Jamieson, J. N. B. Bell, and M. G. Yost, "The effects of electric fields on charged molecules and particles in individual microenvironments," Atmospheric Environment, vol. 41, no. 25, pp. 5224–5235, 2007.

S. J. Genuis, "Fielding a current idea: exploring the public health impact of electromagnetic radiation," Public Health, vol. 122, no. 2, pp. 113–124, 2008.

G. Chevalier, K. Mori, and J. L. Oschman, "The effect of Earthing (grounding) on human physiology," European Biology and Bioelectromagnetics, vol. 2, no. 1, pp. 600–621, 2006.

G. Chevalier, "Changes in pulse rate, respiratory rate, blood oxygenation, perfusion index, skin conductance, and their variability induced during and after grounding human subjects for 40 minutes," Journal of Alternative and Complementary Medicine, vol. 16, no. 1, pp. 1–7, 2010.

R. Brown, G. Chevalier, and M. Hill, "Pilot study on the effect of grounding on delayed-onset muscle soreness," Journal of Alternative and Complementary Medicine, vol. 16, no. 3, pp. 265–273, 2010.

M. F. Bobbert, A. P. Hollander, and P. A. Huijing, "Factors in delayed onset muscular soreness of man," Medicine and Science in Sports and Exercise, vol. 18, no. 1, pp. 75–81, 1986.

B. Tartibian, B. Maleki, and A. Abbasi, "The effects of ingestion of Omega-3 fatty acids on perceived pain and external symptoms of delayed onset muscle soreness in untrained men,"Clinical Journal of Sport Medicine, vol. 19, no. 2, pp. 115–119, 2009.

J. Vaile, S. Halson, N. Gill, and B. Dawson, "Effect of hydrotherapy on the signs and symptoms of delayed onset muscle soreness," European Journal of Applied Physiology, vol. 102, no. 4, pp. 447–455, 2008.

Z. Zainuddin, M. Newton, P. Sacco, and K. Nosaka, "Effects of massage on delayed-onset muscle soreness, swelling, and recovery of muscle function," Journal of Athletic Training, vol. 40, no. 3, pp. 174–180, 2005.

M. Hübscher, L. Vogt, M. Bernhörster, A. Rosenhagen, and W. Banzer, "Effects of acupuncture on symptoms and muscle function in delayed-onset muscle soreness," Journal of Alternative and Complementary Medicine, vol. 14, no. 8, pp. 1011–1016, 2008.

32

G. Chevalier and S. Sinatra, "Emotional stress, heart rate variability, grounding, and improved autonomic tone: clinical applications," Integrative Medicine: A Clinician's Journal, vol. 10, no. 3, 2011.

J. L. Oschman, "Can electrons act as antioxidants? A review and commentary," Journal of Alternative and Complementary Medicine, vol. 13, no. 9, pp. 955–967, 2007.

G. Chevalier, S. T. Sinatra, J. L. Oschman, and R. M. Delany, "Grounding the human body reduces blood viscosity—a major factor in cardiovascular disease," Journal of Alternative and Complementary Medicine. In press.

S. Adak, S. Chowdhury, and M. Bhattacharyya, "Dynamic and electrokinetic behavior of erythrocyte membrane in diabetes mellitus and diabetic cardiovascular disease," Biochimica et Biophysica Acta, vol. 1780, no. 2, pp. 108–115, 2008.

M. Chahine, A. Chatelier, O. Babich, and J. J. Krupp, "Voltage-gated sodium channels in neurological disorders," CNS and Neurological Disorders—Drug Targets, vol. 7, no. 2, pp. 144–158, 2008.

C. Franceschi, M. Bonafè, S. Valensin et al., "Inflamm-aging: an evolutionary perspective on immunosenescence," Annals of the New York Academy of Sciences, vol. 908, pp. 244–254, 2000.

S. de Flora, A. Quaglia, C. Bennicelli, and M. Vercelli, "The epidemiological revolution of the 20th century," FASEB Journal, vol. 19, no. 8, pp. 892–897, 2005.

http://www.soilandhealth.org
http://www.naturalnews.com
http://endoftheamericandream.com
http://www.cancerdefeated.com
http://joannebrophy.com
http://www.computerworlduk.com
http://www.infowars.com http://undergroundhealthreporter.com

33

Chapter 113: Additional Resources

Gnosticism: http://www.earlychristianwritings.com

Gnosticism: http://www.gnosis.org

Rosicrucian Fellowship: http://rosicrucian.com

Freezone Scientology: http://www.freezoneearth.org

Freezone Scientology: http://internationalfreezone.net

The Knights of Solomon: http://knightsofsolomon.org

The Knights of Jerusalem: http://www.smotj.org

The Knights of Christ: http://www.ordendeltemple.org

The Knights of St. John: http://www.orderstjohn.org

American Institute of Physics: http://www.aip.org

History of Science: http://www.todayinsci.com

Book Review Request

Dear Reader,

Thank you for purchasing this book!

I would love to know your opinion.

Writing a book review helps in understanding readers and also has an impact on other reader's purchasing decisions. Your opinion matters.

Please write a book review! Your kindness is greatly appreciated!

Other Books Written By The Author

- 66 Days to Change Your Life: 12 Steps to Effortlessly Remove Mental Blocks, Reprogram Your Brain and Become a Money Magnet

- A New Way of Being: How to Rewire Your Brain and Take Control of Your Life

- Codex Illuminatus: Quotes & Sayings of Dan Desmarques

- Collective Consciousness: How to Transcend Mass Consciousness and Become One With the Universe

- Deception: When Everything You Know about God is Wrong

- Find Your Flow: Find Your Flow: How to Get Wisdom and Knowledge from God

- Holistic Psychology: 77 Secrets about the Mind That They Don't Want You to Know

- How to Change the World: The Path of Global Ascension Through Consciousness

- Psychology: 77 Secrets about the Mind That They Don't Want You to Know

- Religious Leadership: The 8 Rules Behind Successful Congregations

- Spiritual Warfare: What You Need to Know About Overcoming Adversity

- Technocracy: The New World Order of the Illuminati and The Battle Between Good and Evil

- The 10 Laws of Transmutation: The Multidimensional Power of Your Subconscious Mind

- The 14 Karmic Laws of Love: How to Develop a Healthy and Conscious Relationship With Your Soulmate

- The Antichrist: The Grand Plan of Total Global Enslavement Holistic

- The Evil Within: The Spiritual Battle in Your Mind

- The Hidden Language of God: How to Find a Balance Between Freedom and Responsibility

- The Secret Empire: The Hidden Truth Behind the Power Elite and the Knights of the New World Order

- The Secret Science of the Soul: How to Transcend Common Sense and Get What You Really Want From Life

- The Spiritual Mechanics of Love: Secrets They Don't Want You to Know about Understanding and Processing Emotions

- Your Full Potential: How to Overcome Fear and Solve Any Problem

- Your Soul Purpose: Reincarnation and the Spectrum of Consciousness in Human Evolution

- Uncommon: Transcending the Lies of the Mental Health Industry

www.ingramcontent.com/pod-product-compliance
Lightning Source LLC
Chambersburg PA
CBHW071949070526
44583CB00015B/1129